DEATH OF A MAN

DEATH OF A MAN

by Lael Tucker Wertenbaker

BEACON PRESS : BOSTON

To the children of Charles Christian Wertenbaker,
William, Christian, and Timberlake

Library of Congress Cataloging in Publication Data

Wertenbaker, Lael Tucker, 1909–
  Death of a man.
  Reprint of the 1957 ed. published by Random House,
New York; with new introd.
    1. Wertenbaker, Charles, 1901–1955. 2. Wertenbaker,
Lael Tucker, 1909–   I. Title [DNLM. 1. Death —
Personal narratives. 2. Euthanasia — Personal narratives.
W50 W497d 1957F]
[PS3545.E8256Z95 1974]   813'.5'2 [B]   73–16889
ISBN 0–8070–2762–6
ISBN 0–8070–2763–4 (pbk.)

INTRODUCTION

Joseph Fletcher

"Dying is the last thing I'll have a chance to do well," Wert said to Lael when they knew for sure he was going to die soon. "I hope to hell I can."

Good dying (which is what euthanasia means literally) has at last found its place in our scheme of things, along with good birthing, good living, and good loving. After all, it makes sense to strive for quality in everything we do—as much in our dying as in our living. Quality dying as well as living; quality is what we want, all along the human spectrum.

Two decades ago I wrote a book, *Morals and Medicine,* defending euthanasia and the right of patients to know the truth if they wanted to. In 1954, by coincidence the same year in which my book was published, Charles Wertenbaker acted out in fact what I defended in principle. Within another two years his wife, Lael, had written her extraordinary, utterly absorbing account of Wert's life in the perspective of his free man's death. *Death of a Man* was published in 1957.

It is not surprising to me that her book and mine now are being republished by Beacon Press. Twenty years is a very long life for most books, but the subject these books cope with is looming larger than ever in the civilizing story of the morals of men. When something comes close to the quick, as this does—to solemn, universal, bedrock human experience—it does not drop out of sight overnight.

In those twenty years medical techniques for prolonging life have burgeoned. But success has problems, just as much as failure does. Modern medicine has succeeded so well at resuscitating patients whose lives a decade or two ago would have been over and finished, and at artificially supporting human functions like breathing and heartbeat long after they have come to an end spontaneously, that we now find ourselves crossing the line from prolonging their living to actually prolonging their dying. When do we stop the intravenous fluids and remove the nasal and tracheal tubes and turn off the respirators? It's a fallacy, an irrational hang-up, to feel that an increase or stubborn lengthening of life in and of itself is a good thing—just increasing the quantity of life regardless of its quality.

One of the most exciting discoveries or fresh insights of the late twentieth century is what I like to call "the fallacy of increase." We are beginning to see, even though only reluctantly, that growth is not always or necessarily good. This was the impact of the 1970 Club of Rome's warning about the law of diminishing returns as it applies to industrial technology and economic expansion; their report upset the conventional wisdom. But there are indeed limits to growth. In point of fact, John Stuart Mill exposed this fallacy in his essay on "the stationary state" over a hundred years ago; he showed why there is an optimal or nodal point in all developments, a stop sign for those who are sane enough to see it. The fallacy of increase applies as much to death and dying as to anything else.

In *The Doctor's Dilemma* George Bernard Shaw says, "All professions are conspiracies against the laity." And the plain fact is that people nowadays are getting to be more afraid of what the life savers might do to them than of death itself; dehumanized senility is the new specter haunting us. "Dear God," they say, "don't let me go through what happened to poor old helpless Uncle Ed, through all those relentless months and years." Then they try to get their doctors to promise to spare them that kind of end, and the doctors say, legally right but morally wrong, that they can't promise any such thing. This is the true doctor's dilemma; a desire on the one hand to help, out of loving concern, in conflict with an archaic but traditional commitment to a patient's body, even though the patient is gone as a person and cannot ever return.

The two lovers in the Wertenbaker story, *Death of a Man,* were brave and rational and ethical; they understood that quality is better than quantity, that personal integrity outranks mere physical existence, that just being alive, if you cannot be human, is not a gain but a loss. Furthermore, they accepted the reality of death as a part of life. Charles Wertenbaker was a physician's son, Lael Tucker was a clergyman's daughter. Death was a prominent part of their picture as they grew up, in one papa's clinical practice and in the other's religious ministry.

Admittedly this is not the case with most people. A medical reporter recently remarked that death is "our most repressed reality." We sweep it under the cultural rug, repress it. Cemeteries are remote, dying takes place in hospitals rather than at home, "morticians" are eager "to see to everything for you," and even the word death itself is hushed up with silly euphemisms (passed on, gone away, resting, in heaven, and other tricks in the semantics of death).

Wert and Lael were too mature for word games or any of the evasions and devices psychologists call denial maneuvers. As free, proud, and honest human beings they always felt only contempt for Alexander Pope's bourgeois advice to keep up with the Joneses, or back with them:

> Be not the first by whom the new is tried
> Nor yet the last to lay the old aside.

They promptly laid aside the old taboo on suicide when it undermined their human integrity; they were not the first, of course, but certainly among the bravest and frankest. I always remember a shade tree preacher, a poor old West Indian who came every Saturday afternoon to the market place in Frederiksted on St. Croix, to declare the imminence and prevalence of death. The square always quickly emptied of the dawdlers, but not because of his manners so much as because of his message. Most of the time it's easier to heed the first part only of the wisdom of Ecclesiastes: "There is a time to live and a time to die."

To talk about a "time to die" and *good dying* we have to watch out for the traps of semantics. Words can be either weapons or false faces. The law has been so stern on the subject of suicide that courts have had to sidestep the issue in the few cases they were unable to keep off their dockets. They've done it by getting around the law itself with verdicts "while of unsound mind" or "temporary insanity." Back when the word euthanasia was thought to have only an active or positive meaning, the sense of actually doing something to end suffering and dehumanization, the Euthanasia Society of America enlisted only a very few activists. The idea offended too many taboos, ancient religious feelings about the sanctity or even the sacro-sanctity of life. *Death of a Man* was called "Greek" in its attitudes — even though the Greeks too were divided about suicide or any other human initiative in dying. Still, Pythagoras and Plato and Aristotle all voted for euthanasia —

death induced for reasons of mercy and dignity. Valerius Maximus said it was the policy of the magistrates in Marseilles to keep a supply of poison on hand for those who could give a good reason to die. Compare this compassion to what we read in the story of Charles Wertenbaker's search for the *coup de grâce*.

People in our own times finally began to face up to the problem of quality dying when medicine's ability to keep terminal patients "going" forced them to ask when the cutoff point comes. When should we at least stop preserving life, even if we suppose we cannot directly end it? When may we contrive death for ourselves or others, by omission, even if we cannot contrive it by commission?

By the summer of 1973 the Euthanasia Society's office was filing 500 requests per week for "living wills"—formal but legally unenforceable requests to the signer's family, clergyman, and lawyer that the signer be allowed to die whenever there was no reasonable expectation of recovering from an illness. In 1973 the legislatures of two states, Florida and Oregon, voted down bills to permit medical and personal discretion about when to stop life support; but both bills had solid backing, signaling the slow and nervous progress of a conflicted social conscience toward social sanity. A year earlier a Senate Special Committee on Aging heard testimony in favor of letting patients go ("passive euthanasia"); its published official record carried the title *Death with Dignity*.

The popular notion is that *elective* death is morally all right if you elect to stop fighting it off but morally wrong if you elect to facilitate it. This shifts the focus from a positive reasonable decision to terminate hopeless suffering to a negative or passive acceptance of death that comes on its own terms, without further struggle.

This is only a part, only the negative part, of the Society's original message. Still, short-term gains are always attractive, even at the expense of long-term gains. At least the public was beginning to realize that sometimes we should be allowed to die without further meddling. Since people generally are not ready to approve the exercise of human initiative in death (they approve birth control but not death control), prudence seemed to call for the soft pedal. The Society began to use the soft pedal. Some of the doctors on its board have even been heard to say they would resign if the Society's historic aim is revived — even if it were only another *option* in dealing with terminal illness. One of them is reported as refusing even to let the subject be discussed. Passive euthanasia only, they say. Some have even urged that the word euthanasia itself be dropped because of its historic associations.

Death of a Man is the story, on the other hand, of authentic and sturdy euthanasia — direct, not indirect; positive, not negative; active, not passive; responsible, not fatalistic. Wert and Lael never wanted him to lie down, to wait willy-nilly for death to come in its own way, in its own time, and on its own terms. They chose to go out to meet it and to usher it in, as a visitor who could not be denied but could at least be controlled. Wert was a victor, not merely a victim.

There are at bottom three questions at stake in the problem of dealing with terminal illness ethically. First, ought we to stop trying to preserve a patient's life in certain cases? The indirect, passive policy which has largely taken over in the Society and in hospitals gives a Yes answer to this. Second, ought we actually and purposefully to hasten a patient's death in certain cases? The direct, active ethic dramatized by the Wertenbakers gives a Yes answer to this. It is important to note that they could logically also give a Yes answer to the first question as well (either tactic, depending on the situation), but that the indirect passivity policy could not say Yes to the second question — not even selectively or with situational flexibility.

The third question is, when has death really come; how are we to know and determine that it has? The main issue here is between those who contend that death is systemic, that it occurs only when spontaneous functions like breathing, blood circulation, and heart-beat have ended irreversibly, on the one hand, and a newly emerging view that the patient as a person is dead when cerebral (mental) function is at an end, no matter and even if other biological and neurological functions continue — in short, patients who have become the equivalent of vegetables.

This third question is somewhat off our path and cannot be properly treated here. Yet it surfaces once or twice in Lael's book. For example, Wert in his memoir, when he considered swimming outside the harbor at St. Jean-de-Luz until he drowned, says something about wanting to avoid "becoming a patient instead of a person."

But surely his language was off the beam at that point. Any patient is a person, no matter how helpless and hurt, until he is irreversibly or incorrigibly comatose. In that case, in the view I would want to defend, the patient — the person — is gone, is already dead, and only a body is left. But there are also times, as Wert understood, when we would be right to end the life of a patient (person) — still with his full faculties. This is the euthanasia ethic. The thrust of the definition of truly *human* life in terms of cerebration is that excerebrates are already dead; the thrust of euthanasia is that those who are still alive may morally choose to end their lives when the flame is no longer worth the candle.

It should be obvious that the question "What is a human being — what is humanness?" has an important bearing; yet the main issue raised by *Death of a Man* is the one about direct-versus-indirect euthanasia. The problem is a worrisome one for society as well as for medical ethics, now that longevity is so greatly increased and so many people live to a ripe old age when chronic and degenerative maladies start to plague them. (Just in this century the average life span has gone from 40 years to 70.)

Indiscriminate "life saving" by the staff of intensive care units can be cruel and inhuman. But to dampen down the compulsive, undiscriminating life saver only meets a part of the whole problem. It is nothing more than indirect euthanasia, of the living will variety. In fact, it is at most a sort of grudging or half-baked sympathy for the dying — what the Victorian poet Arthur Clough expressed:

> *Thou shalt not kill, yet need not strive*
> *Officiously to keep alive.*

A recent Harris poll found that 62 percent of the public believed that a terminal patient ought to be allowed to die, and only 28 percent would say it is wrong to stop treatment. On the other hand, although 53 percent opposed direct euthanasia, 37 percent favored it — an impressively large, and enlarged, number.

Here, then, is the real issue. Arguing about passive euthanasia is flogging a dead horse. Even Ann Landers, the syndicated genius of instant morality, endorses it. In a higher bracket of the establishment, the American Hospital Association does too. The courts have upheld it with increasing frequency in their decrees and verdicts. After all, the requirement of a patient's consent to treatment (hospital waivers) plainly implies that people may not be compelled to go on living. Neither is it any longer a malpractice bugaboo in medical circles.

As far as moral philosophy is concerned, the major issue has to do with the relation of means and ends. Some of us (consequentialists) hold that only the end sought in any act gives it justification; its purpose is its meaning and its value. Otherwise, without an end or purpose, our actions are meaningless and amoral. The nub of this ethics is that the end justifies the means — although it does not mean, of course, that *any* end can justify *any* means. Between them there must be some sensible proportion, some relative value. The real question is not whether the end justifies the means (nothing else can) but *what justifies the end?*

People in the other camp contend that there is also an ethics of means, independent of ends, and that some things are a priori always wrong regardless of how much good might follow from doing them. The religious mafia that calls itself a Right-to-Life movement, agitating for a prohibitionist policy on both abortion and euthanasia, holds that it is always intrinsically wrong to end an innocent life, whether it is prepersonal, personal, or postpersonal, and regardless of the good to be gained. Ends or values, such as human dignity, compassion, and dislike of useless suffering, are, say the mafia, irrelevant.

In the euthanasia debate some of the opposition opt for a passive or indirect ending of terminal patients' lives. They are not quite as life-crazy as some of the more radical vitalists in the mafia. I even know a few who would not only let some patients go without offering further life-support, they would not even — for example — join the rest of the mafia in artificially supporting the life of a hopelessly brain-crushed pregnant schoolgirl, for say seven months, until a month-long embryo in her womb could be brought to delivery alive or, as they might say, "to save the baby."

But the main point is that both forms of euthanasia, direct and indirect, are seeking the same end. Only the means are different— the same strategy but different tactics. In one form the goal is achieved simply by omission, doing nothing; in the other, by commission, doing something. Thus the crucial question is: If the end is good (in this case release from a degrading death) why not use whatever means best bring us to the good? Provided, we might add, that in doing so we would not be victimizing others. Kant said that if we will the end we will the means. We should use whatever means is appropriate to our goal, if and when there is a benefit proportionate to the cost.

Wert was as shrewd as any moral philosopher when he said to Lael, "It's damned hard to tell right from wrong, but it's easy to tell good from evil." Tricky indeed is the business of trying to decide which general ethical principle applies in a particular situation and which one doesn't; for example, figuring out when or at what point we have crossed the line from prolonging life to simply prolonging death. It is not always easy to decide when and who and how we can die with dignity, with freedom and responsibility — rather than blindly and fatalistically submitting to brute end-stage processes of collapse. But it isn't by any means so tricky, if you have a mature sense of values, to tell that suffering or coma or dehumanization by drugs and analgesia is bad, and that the liberty of choosing to die in possession of one's own selfhood as a person, still able to say good-bye to one's loved ones and then to go, is good.

Not everybody is mature or morally secure enough to choose to die. Nobody should be compelled to choose — as Socrates was, for his neglect of religious rules. Compulsion and choice are mutually exclusive. On the other hand, nobody should be compelled *not* to choose. With some people (but not all) their beliefs about another life after death might have a lot to do with their attitude toward dying. Strangely enough, some who believe or believe they believe in immortality cling frantically and abjectly to their mortal life. This contrasts with a quiet acceptance of the prospect of nonbeing by those who believe that death is the end, saying with Lucretius, "Where I am, death is not; where death is, I am not: why, then, fear death?"

Men and women die well or badly by many creeds. The issue is ethical, not theological or psychological. It is one that requires great consideration while there is time to consider it for oneself. To truly acknowledge death as the end of this life, which it is, is not to diminish life but to enhance it. Wert took the matter and manner of his dying into his own hands. In their acceptance of his imminent death Wert and Lael were able to share many hours that Wert said were "the best of a lifetime."

I

I learned that I had cancer at 3:45 in the afternoon of Monday, September 27, 1954, in the plainly furnished office of a radiologist just off the Rue Gambetta in St. Jean-de-Luz, France. I have been precise about the time and place because I have had to be arbitrary about the fact itself. I could say that I had known it, obscurely, for at least a year, but the suspicion, at times amounting to a conviction, that had occasionally come over me had never been persistent enough to cause me to put it to the test; in spite of recurrent abdominal pains, on the whole I had felt too well. I could say that I didn't know it, positively, until after my operation, but before then the doctors I saw had given up more than a half-hearted pretense that it might be something else. And so I choose that hour of 3:45 Monday, when X rays had confirmed the existence of a growth that I had been able to feel with my fingers—a lump about the size of a golf ball, I judged, which Dr. Cartier had hopefully assured me *might* be a spasm, a knot, or something else besides the thing he would not mention by name. For ten days, Dr. Cartier, a cautious, gentle

3

man (the name is not his real one, nor are the names of the other doctors in this report), had been examining me for an intestinal disorder and had had me on a diet and on the wagon. As my other symptoms decreased, there remained that small knot on the right side of my abdomen. He prescribed a fluoroscopic examination and X rays and I was examined by Dr. Cartier himself and by the radiologist, a confident young man named Barcet, on Saturday morning, September 25. The examination was incomplete; I could not retain the barium, fed from below, and so only the second half of the large intestinal tract could be seen. This indicated to me that something was badly wrong up above, as did the muttered conversation of the two doctors, the conversation of technical men over a technical problem, which I might overhear but could not understand much of, in French. But when, leaving Dr. Barcet's office, I came out with the word cancer to Dr. Cartier, he put his hand on my arm and assured me that it was most unlikely; there were no signs right up to the very edge of the suspicious spot, which barium couldn't reach. On Monday, having breakfasted on barium, I went to Dr. Barcet's office at noon, and he made the examination alone. It did not take him long. I asked him if he had found what he was looking for, and he said yes. He told me to come back at three o'clock, when Dr. Cartier would be there. Then, after a brief hesitation, he changed the time to 3:15; Dr. Cartier, he explained, was coming at three on another case. This should have told me that he wanted to talk to Dr.

Cartier before seeing me—and so it did, but I was slow in assimilating the information. It didn't register until after I had met the two doctors, submitted to another brief X ray—possibly to keep me occupied—and, after dressing, stepped out into the waiting room to find Dr. Cartier in sober conversation with my wife, who had gone with me on all my visits. She turned to me and said quickly: "This is pretty serious," and then, of course, I knew. From a reporter's habit, I glanced at my watch. It was 3:45.

A few days earlier, I had had a long discussion with my wife about one aspect of the situation that troubled me: the reluctance of many doctors to tell a patient an unpleasant truth. Ever since I can remember, it had seemed to me that to be deceived about the nature or progress of a serious illness, or even to suspect deceit, would go far toward destroying whatever fortitude one could summon to face one's trials. My wife had agreed with me immediately. "To tell you anything less than the whole truth would be to try to reduce you," she said. "I promise you I will never do that." Neither of us then suspected how much pressure she would have to resist to keep that promise; the first indication of it came to her just before I walked from the examination room into the waiting room that Monday afternoon. Dr. Cartier, a worried look on his handsome face, asked her how much he should tell me. "Tell him everything," she said.

He could not bring himself to do so yet. Dr. Cartier, the vigor of whose middle age was being nibbled away by asthma, was a kind and sensitive man. When I turned to him for an explanation of my wife's words, "pretty serious," he said only: "You'll have to have an operation." I sat down at the small round table where he and my wife had drawn up chairs—the ubiquitous waiting-room table piled with old magazines—and lit a cigarette, waiting for him to be more informative. He drew to the center of the table a large X-ray photograph, still wet, of a whitened labyrinth, and pointed out to me a dark area that plainly didn't belong there, partially eclipsing a curve of the large intestine, just beyond where the small intestine joined it. Then he explained that this *"chose,"* as he called it, was well placed, easily accessible, near the outer wall of the abdomen; it would be a fairly simple matter to remove it, he said. I interrupted to speak the forbidden word again: if it was cancer, what about the—what were they called?—tentacles?—and I illustrated by drawing an octopus on the table top with my finger (baby octopi, or *chiperones,* are a gastronomic delicacy in the region of St. Jean-de-Luz). Dr. Cartier heartily assured me that it was by no means certain that this was malignant (*mauvaise* was the word he used); many tumors were not *mauvaise,* and there was no indication of metastasis—the word I had wanted for spreading. But it was necessary to hurry, to take this while it was young; he advised me to wait no more than three or four days. He recommended a surgeon who had a clinic in Bayonne, the largest city in this part of France, fifteen miles away, and offered to make an appointment for a consultation

6

the next afternoon. I agreed to the consultation, then, as we got up to leave, I asked him point-blank: "If I do nothing about this, how long will I live?" A look of shock passed over his face, and, as he had done the other time, he took my arm. "But that would be foolish," he said. I told him that I was only trying to consider all the possibilities. After another moment, he answered: "Perhaps a year, perhaps two years—if it is *mauvaise*."

We said "until tomorrow" to Dr. Cartier outside his office, across the narrow Rue Gambetta, and walked two blocks to the beach, which was almost deserted since the swimming had ended with the equinoctial storms of the previous week. More people were strolling along the flower-bordered walk above the beach, but there were fewer tourists than local people, who could be identified by their everyday clothes; now that the season was over, almost everybody had time for a walk. We walked as far as the sidewalk took us, nearly half a mile to the end of the beige crescent, where we could hear the sea pounding the outer breakwater, then we turned and started back. All the way I felt my wife in step beside me, but neither of us had spoken yet.

Before we talked about the immediate problems—as she knew—I needed to come to terms with what I had learned. Dr. Cartier's manner had told me more than his words, and I was in no doubt of what I had—or perhaps there still lingered a ten percent doubt, which was about what I guessed him to have. My father had died of cancer at fifty-seven; his

7

mother had died of cancer in her sixties; his brother in his sixties; there was cancer in my mother's family, too. I had expected to get it some day—one usually got a fatal disease some day—but I hadn't looked for it at fifty-three. And yet those frequent pains had been warning me of something for nearly eighteen months. A year or so ago I had called Dr. Cartier, who had felt about and found nothing out of order. He said then that I must diet for ten days before he could make a complete examination; meanwhile, four or five days without rich food or strong drink had made me feel as good as new. So I had concluded that rich meals and more than a moderate amount of alcohol were things that I had better learn to take less often, and for the time being had gone on taking them as often as I pleased. Walking beside the beach that day, in a fresh breeze from the sea, I remembered many times, usually driving home in discomfort after a fine, big meal, that the word "cancer" had come into my mind and given me a chill of fear. But the very thing that might have been expected to help me helped instead to deceive me. I am something of a hypochondriac. Many times I have imagined that I was getting pneumonia when all I had was a cold, and my imagination has conjured many a cut finger into blood poisoning. Conversely, the only time in recent years that I had a serious illness—scarlet fever—I treated it as flu, got up after three days, and had complications for half a year. And so it was pretty much in character both that I should have scares and that I should treat them too lightly afterwards. Each time

I had had one of those cancer scares, I had made a deal with myself; I would call Dr. Cartier only when I was willing to submit to his diet for ten days. Exactly ten days ago, after a farewell dinner for some vacationing friends, I had called him. Now there was no use in wishing that I had acted otherwise; I must decide how to act from now on.

The first question, of course, was about the operation—whether to have it in France or go home. To let my wife know that I had settled for the situation, at least for the present, I said: "This is going to cost some money, any way we do it."

"That's not important," she said.

Except for two periods at home, one of a year, the other of two and a half, we had been living in France since we had come as correspondents in 1944. Since 1947 we had lived just across the mouth of the Nivelle River from St. Jean-de-Luz, in the non-resort, fishermen's town of Ciboure, and we had established a life that we valued. For our children—boy of eleven, girl of eight, both bilingual—it was the small-town life hard to find in America nowadays, plus a better grade-school education than we could have afforded for them at home; for ourselves, it was a more comfortable, a more tranquil life than we could have lived in America on the income from books and some magazine work. But there was no allowance in our budget for a major operation, with weeks in a hospital and more weeks of convalescence, and certainly none to take two of us to New York and back. We did have a savings account for emergencies, and this seemed to be one, but I wasn't too confident that the account would outlast the emergency. "If we decide to have this done in New York," I said, "I think I'd better go alone."

And my wife said: "Wherever it's done, I'm going with you."

I put up no argument. I knew that my wife could leave the children with Madame Sueur, our landlady, housekeeper, cook, banker, everything, and worry about them hardly at all. As for the expense, if she could afford it, I could; I wanted her along. We discovered that we were both thinking of the same doctor for the operation—Dr. James Danielson, who was chief surgeon at one of the big New York hospitals, who had performed a delicate operation on our son when Chris was three, and who, besides, was an old friend of my wife's. And we discovered that we both wanted him chiefly for the last reason: as an old friend, he would have to tell her all there was to tell—and she, of course, would tell me. We reminded each other that, no matter how highly regarded the Bayonne surgeon might be, Bayonne was a city of only about twenty thousand, and this was a serious matter to trust to a provincial doctor. We agreed that we had better have the consultation; it would be a check on Dr. Cartier's diagnosis; but that unless we were greatly impressed by the surgeon, we would cable Danielson and fly home. We could be ready to leave by Thursday.

That night my wife sat up with me until my bedtime,

which was long past hers, but beyond the practicalities of getting home, I don't remember what we talked about; of the central subject there was so little to be said. The next afternoon we drove to Bayonne with Dr. Cartier, and in the operating room of a neat, new clinic Dr. Delbos, a small man with a scar across his cheek, examined the X rays and me, doing both with dispatch. He agreed with Dr. Cartier that I must have an operation at once, and, like Dr. Cartier, he remarked that "it" was well placed. I asked him whether in his opinion "it" was definitely cancer, but he avoided a direct answer; whatever it was, he said, it must come out. I mentioned that there had been a great deal of cancer in my family, and he said: "That is true of all Frenchmen. I suppose it is also true of Americans." I liked his manner and his movements, both of which had assurance, but I said to him only that I would let him know within twenty-four hours whether I would call on him for his services or go to New York. He nodded and went about his other business, and I paid his head nurse a thousand francs and we left. Walking across the courtyard to the car, under a spreading tree, Dr. Cartier stooped and picked up a horse chestnut and began polishing it on his sleeve. I remembered the polished horse chestnuts of my boyhood, but I am unable to say whether this had anything to do with my decision, given to my wife as soon as we had left Dr. Cartier and were having tea at the Bar Basque, to go home for what had to be done.

If, I silently amended, I was decided that it had to be done.

That night I persuaded my wife to go to bed at her usual hour, and I sat up alone, rationing myself gum drops in lieu of whiskey and going over a sort of semi-decision I had made some time ago. I loved the water where we swam—not at the St. Jean-de-Luz beach, crowded with rows of cabañas, but from another one-tenth its size below an old fort at the dead end of the fishing village of Socoa, opposite St. Jean in the harbor. I could see this beach from the small tower where I worked, on the hilltop above our house, and looking out there, across the blue water where I swam and floated, I had often thought that the most nearly agreeable way to die would be by drowning—drowning in the sight of a well-loved shore, in familiar, well-loved water. (And I don't think the likeness to the womb of this vision had much to do with its attraction.) Lately, as thoughts of cancer had occupied more of my mind, the vision had become more personal; I had imagined myself swimming far out into the harbor, and through the channel between the breakwaters to the open sea, and there, floating on my back, taking a last look at the bright crescent of shore spotted with pink-tile-roofed houses, floating in the buoyant water as long as I liked, until, the moment come, I lowered my head and filled my lungs with water; I had imagined that then all the good things of my life would come before me, the bad things blotted out, and that I would take them with me into the final nothingness. Now, alone at night, it seemed to me that this was the only fitting course, the only quick, clean way out of my predicament. The alternative was hospitals, pain, becoming a patient instead of a person, and probably the same result in the end—only by then I would be reduced to something less than a man who could swim out to meet his death. But could I? And what was more important than the question of courage: should I, until I had exhausted all my chances? Many cancers had been successfully removed; I had known people who had had them out and who had seemed not much the worse for it. So my mind went back and forth, but when I went to bed it was with the feeling, rather than the reasoned conviction, that I had better take that swim in the morning.

The weather might have been conspiring with me. When I finished breakfast, around 10:30, the sky was clear, the wind had died, the sun was bright, and there was only the faintest tang of autumn in the air. By noon even that should be gone. Before going to my tower to sort out some papers, I put on a bikini and the jersey and trousers I usually wore to the beach, and outside the front door I called to my wife upstairs to tell her that I might go swimming later. She put her head out the window and said she had to leave for Biarritz at noon to pick up our train and airplane tickets; if I was ready any time before that, she could drive me down. So luck was in the conspiracy. She would not be with me, and it was unlikely that anybody else would be on the little beach. In the tower, I made short work of my papers, filling a manila envelope with what I would take with me, leaving the rest in other envelopes, marked so that my wife could decide what to destroy and what was worth keeping for a while.

In the date book he carried in his pocket, Charles Christian Wertenbaker wrote, under *mercredi 29 Septembre*: "No swim."

2

Charles Christian Wertenbaker outlined and began to write, while he was dying, a short book which he titled *Sixty Days in a Lifetime*. There was a parenthetical question mark beside the title suggesting that he might have changed it. Part I, *The Octopus* ("a factual, objective report on what happened from X rays to date, with cutbacks, and some reflection to dispose of 'most of my follies were committed in my twenties, most of my sins in my thirties,' and why no need to recall them"), he completed only through the words "and what was worth keeping for a while." The other two parts were to have been *A Virginia Childhood,* and *A Rainbow on Gibraltar* ("the story of my life and hubris. This is search for the essence of perfection in this marriage, and tell it as a search").

The outline, some notes, and the opening pages were handwritten on a long, yellow, ruled pad. I also have the neat, brief notes he made daily in his small, brown-leather-covered date book. My husband's—Wert's—handwriting was strong, middle-sized, and clear, with a slight flourish only about the *t's*. He was a truthful and accurate man.

I cannot hope to write what he was unable to finish. I can write nothing of his boyhood, which I only know about from him. I cannot write the things he would have written of our marriage and our years together. I am not as factually accurate and objective nor as much of a writer as he was, but

I shall try to tell what happened from September 27th on as objectively and accurately as I can, because in the perspective of death he looked closely at living and evaluated it. The two words we used most often were "important" and "unimportant" as death made these categories very clear to us. I shall try to be as truthful as he was, which is important.

In going through the papers he left in the tower, I came across a few notes that belong with this. One, made in April, five months before the first X rays were taken, illuminates his consideration of the swim to death and belongs in here now. "Problem with death is to recognize the point at which you can die with all your faculties, take a healthy look at the world and people as you go out of it. Let them get you in bed, drug you or cut you, and you become sick and afraid and disgusting, and everybody will be glad to get rid of you. It shouldn't be such a problem if you can remember how it was when you were young. You wouldn't give up something for instance to add ten years to your life. All right, don't ask for them now. You wouldn't give up drinking and love-making and eating—and why should you have given them up? Nothing is ever lost that has been experienced and it can all be there at the moment of death—if you don't wait too long."

It was a principle with him, a moral and principled man, that he had a right to die as he wished to, when he chose, if possible. I believe this, too. We talked about this later, as we talked about everything else. If he had taken that swim, I would have understood it, which he knew. I would have been sure, furthermore, that he was doomed by the cancer and knew it in the somber places of his deep intuitions. This would have been an unreasonable faith in him, and therefore difficult to convey to his children. That was one reason for his decision not to swim; that, and, among other reasons, his feeling that he owed his manhood a test of pain, the bearing of pain, before he died. He had suffered comparatively little physical pain in his life. There was also, in his decision, the very small chance he felt that he might survive whole and well. Wert had great zest and love for living.

When I went ahead of him to bed that Tuesday night, I was aware what was in his mind. As in the few other times in our life together when he had to make a final decision alone, it seemed to me the only way to express my faith in him was to sleep, to have him find me sleeping when he came to bed. It did not matter how important to me his decision was—it was his. My confidence was his.

Wednesday was full of chores: the tickets for Thursday to get and pay for in Biarritz; my two suits, already ordered, to pick up in San Sebastián, just across the border in Spain, for I had bought no city clothes for seven years and would need them in New York as I had thought to need them for a trip we hoped to make later to Madrid and Barcelona; packing; and a last-minute talk with Madame Sueur "in case."

Our household was used to our departures, planned or sudden. We once decided to go for several days to Zaragoza, Spain, at four o'clock in the afternoon and left at five. The happy arrangements that left our children continuing a busy, school-filled or play-filled village life, with their many friends, and the loving care of Madame for their security, made our goodbyes as perfunctory as our returns were gala and warm. That this trip was more serious the children were conscious, but they were not very troubled. Pop had to have an operation. Operations were unpleasant, but lots of people had them, usually at the local clinic on the Quai Ravel in Ciboure. Sometimes Madame took the children to see convalescing friends in Ciboure or St. Jean-de-Luz. Chris had had an operation himself, a long time ago. The scar on his belly did not distress him. I had been with him when he went out and when he waked up, which he remembered. Daughter Timberlake was worried most because Pop could not eat and drink heartily: "Poor Pop. He does love to eat and drink." "After," son Chris told her.

There was a cantaloupe in the icebox. When I was ready

to leave the house on my errands I cut it and it was perfect—small, tart, with deeply tinted stiff flesh, and sweet. Wert could eat that, so I took it up with me to the tower with a spoon in it. After giving the signal on the horn of the car, I waited. Wert usually had a sentence to finish before he came out on the balcony in response to the signal. There was no rattle of typewriter keys this time. The door to the balcony creaked, out of sight, on the bay side of the tower, and then Wert sauntered around the corner and leaned on the balcony rail and looked down at me in the open car. He was wearing one of the wide-striped blue and white French sailor's jerseys he loved and stiff blue fisherman's trousers and dark blue rope-soled sandals. Janet Flanner of the *New Yorker* wrote me later: ". . . a handsome man, it must be a pleasure in itself to be as handsome as he was." A sturdy Basque huntsman said to me, in the mountains near Sare, a year later: "I always remember your husband. He was a very beautiful man."

I am not sure just how handsome he was. He liked it when I teased him and told him he was not, that it was an illusion, that he fooled everyone. His features were odd. His face was markedly asymmetrical. His forehead was disproportionately high. He looked, at a glance, older than his fifty-three years. His mustache was nearly white and his gray hair was cropped so short you could not tell how bald he was. His blue-gray eyes blinked a lot, from old trouble with conjunctivitis, and his mouth was made up of an enormous upper lip, embellished by a trimmed mustache, and a thin lower one. He was tall, with good shoulders and thin, elegant legs, a little too short for his torso. He was not always able to keep his paunch flat. He had fine, soft skin which bronzed deeply in the sun, and the most perfect eyebrows. But it was his deliberate, plenty-of-time-of-day way of moving, his slumbrous, ageless vitality, his sense of the decorativeness becoming to a man, his air of knowing who he was, who you were, his grace, that made him such a pleasure to look at. It nearly always gave me pleasure to look at him, except those few times when I was so angry with him I should have liked to see him defaced. It gave me sharp pleasure now, and he knew it. I understood how he might want to die now, arrogantly, looking like that.

"Be right down," he said, in his double-bass growl. I nodded and held up the melon and he smiled, waved, turned, and sauntered back inside.

The little white tower had a warped red door and locked with an enormous iron key that turned with difficulty in the rusty lock. I saw that the effort of locking it had made him sweat.

"I'm getting mighty weak all of a sudden," Wert remarked, getting into the car.

"I'll call Irwin this afternoon and ask him to meet us in Paris," I said.

Irwin and Marion Shaw lived in St. Jean-de-Luz through the summer months, on a high place behind the town with a view of the countryside matched only from Wert's tower. Irwin had been startled and worried when Wert went on the wagon and on a diet just before they left St. Jean and had telephoned twice from Paris to ask how he was. I had not called back since we had found out that it was serious and not just Wert's overindulgences reflected in the intestinal tract. I had cabled to Dr. Danielson in New York and telephoned to Cook's in Biarritz in the late afternoon of yesterday. Cook's had made the travel reservations for us and Jim Danielson had replied that he would be ready for Wert at the hospital. Wert had asked me if I wanted to cable our oldest friends, Suzie and Charlie Gleaves, in New York, for a bed for myself when we got there, but it seemed to me unnecessary. I could always find a bed. It seemed to me important to act very simply, alarm no one, and to do nothing unimportant. Wert had insisted I pick up my suits, as, indeed, he had insisted before that I have them made. "Armor," he had said yesterday, "new clothes. You'll need them. Besides, otherwise you'll pack a lot of old crap." It was minimum economy to keep our baggage weight down, but I realized now that even the pounds allowed us in the price of the tickets would be too heavy for Wert if, as was likely, there were no porters in Paris. So I would call on the massive strength and friendship of Irwin Shaw to see us from train to plane.

We drove in the brilliant sunshine down the short hill from the tower and turned sharply in the space in front of our small, old, thick-walled villa. Christian Wertenbaker and Begnat Toyos and Timberlake Wertenbaker and Baba Ituria were perched in the tree in front of the house. Basques live by seasons and do not swim in late September, even at noon in a hot sun. Our children did not wish to leave their friends behind in order to enjoy a swim. They waved and we waved back. Driving on down our hill onto the main road, we saw the changed season in the bareness of the blackberry bushes, in the absence of traffic on the highway, in the subtly whipped and lightened color of the bay. We passed the graceful cemetery that curved up the next hill below ours and crossed the bridge over the River Unxin to Socoa. Margot's Bar and Restaurant was the last building at the edge of the narrow, shelf-like road that curled out beside the basin of water where a number of fishing boats lay half-keeled over in the low tide. Months ago one of Wert's recurrent gut-aches had been blamed on her rich *ttoro,* the local fish soup. Last night, as I went to bed, I had said to Wert that I could still hope it was not cancer. Wert had said he was sure it was. I had said, then, allowing for even my natural optimism, that both doctors had certainly sounded positive an operation now would prove successful. Wert had said mmmm.

"I'll be back in time to pick you up," I said as we drove through the arched portal gate over the road that led past the fort and out onto the breakwater.

"No hurry. Drive carefully," said Wert. Then he said, his voice full of joy, "There's nothing we have to say. We've said it all."

There was no one there, at the beach, so we kissed each other. As I turned the car around, a maneuver foreshortened by the psychological hazard of an unprotected twelve-foot drop to the beach, Wert ambled down the path to the sand. In his neat, leisurely manner he laid out the striped beach towel in the spot by a rock we always used, stripped to his bikini, put his wrist watch in one espadrille, folded his clothes, and lay down, full length, his face to the sun. I found myself thinking, as I often had, that he was one of the very few people who could wear a bikini gracefully. I remember all of this very clearly. Driving off, I tried not to hurry.

When I got back and saw him, lying face down this time, wet from the bay, I realized how much I had hoped he would not swim out.

I sat on the sand with my back against the rock until he was ready to leave. One of the felicitous aspects of our life with Madame Sueur was that she did not care what time we ate. In return for this we did not criticize her cooking, which was careless.

"If I die in New York, what will you do?" asked Wert.

"Leave our relatives to take care of your remains," I said without stopping to think about it, "and take the next plane back to the kids. They're what would be important then."

"Good!" said Wert.

I knew he wanted to talk about it and that he did not want me to say "you won't die," or anything of the sort, however much I believed it. He liked making plans, and changing them, and making others. He liked being orderly. It was a basis for behaving spontaneously, when the time came. He was never unduly committed to his plans, but they were usually well-thought-out and ready to be implemented when he chose to follow one. It had taken me quite a while, when we were first married, to realize that he had not committed himself even when he made the most detailed plans. Sometimes this was a nuisance when I found that I had accommodated myself to a course of action we never followed. I came to value this flexibility when I realized how much we might have missed otherwise, either by lack of forethought or by insisting on any preconceived plan.

"I'd like, I think, to be buried in good earth," said Wert. "Or to feed fishes. Go back and enrich sea or land. If you don't mind."

We talked about this a little bit. It was not morbid, the way we talked about it. Rather, it was like the discussions we had had on the shape and placement of the balcony we wanted to build on our reconstructed stable of a house in Sneden's Landing, New York, someday. A discussion without immediacy. He would like to lay his bones in Virginia, where his ancestors were, about whom he was both proud and wry; or in Sneden's Landing, where we owned the only earth we owned and where we had spent our best time together in the United States; or in Ciboure, where we had spent the best of our years; or in the sea. Then we talked about the trip over, for which I had schedule and tickets, and got up and left the beach to go and prepare for the trip. Our passports were always in order.

My talk with Madame—"Ama," we usually called her, as the children did, which is Basque for Mama—was brief. Arrangements had been made "in case" before our other frequent trips away. Our wills were simple enough: everything to me if Wert died; everything to him if I did; our children and our worldly goods to my sister, Julie, if we both did. We felt good about Julie as guardian. She was younger, the fourth of my sisters, happily married to a man we both liked and respected, with a son of her own, and a heart that already loved and wanted our children, the additional ones she'd never had. So that was as all right as possible. I'd written Julie long ago the little there was to say "in case," and that Ama would love and care for Chris and Timberlake in any interval. I always left a note with Ama of roughly how much we owed her at the moment of our departures. Julie would pay her, without questioning her honesty, which was absolute, any further sums she expended. We had not needed to discuss money, Ama and I, in years, except to borrow cash from each other or to settle up once in a while.

This time I said to her, "If Pop should die in New York . . ."

"It's not as serious as that," said Ama firmly.

"No, but listen . . ." I was insistent, for we women were both optimists, but I wanted to get this one thing straight "in case." ". . . *If,* I want you to see that Chris and Timberlake do not suspect it until I get here. I'll cable you and you only and I'll get here within twenty-four hours if I can. It might be in the Paris *Herald Tribune,* so be sure and keep the newspapers out of sight until I get here. I want to be with them and to tell them myself, if."

She agreed and I repeated these instructions to underline them. Repetition is the Basques' method of emphasis, since they say everything with equal positiveness the first time. Then she said: "Listen. Monsieur must get well. He must get *well* well. You must not worry. I will keep the children here for as long as you need to stay in New York for only the rent. I want to do this. I will feed them and clothe them and pay everything. So go for as long as you like and do not worry until Monsieur is well."

Then I telephoned Irwin and his voice boomed down from Paris. "Cancer! My God. Do you need any money? Sure? Well, you know where you can get it if you do. I'll be at the station. Anything else I can do? Anything at all."

That night we went to bed at midnight, early for Wert, together. We were embarked on a course of action for the moment and everything was done and said that made any difference to that course. Weary, and suddenly very weak as he was, Wert made love to me that night. It was simple and mutual and profound.

I think Wert would have written as much. He would have written about it in his way. I don't think it is a violation of the privacy we both valued so highly. We had tried to find the best way of living as we were now to try to find the best way to live with death. How to write about it is a problem because we both happened to be writing people. He could not finish what he wanted to write.

In an unfinished novel he had put aside in which Wert used our marriage as a basis for understanding his fictional married couple, he wrote: "As much from instinct as through her working intelligence, she had understood when she married him that to keep him, and keep him satisfied, she must appeal in more than a negative way to his pride, to his sense of inner decorum, to his feeling that an extramarital affair, like lying, was 'messy'; she had to be the proof, in her own physical person, that fidelity held the ultimate satisfactions. And this had taken the primary effort out of the realm of the physical, applying it to the achievement of a relationship intellectually, ethically, and intuitively so harmonious that the physical meetings became a celebration of the harmony already established."

We slept that night, as we usually did, winter or summer, in close contact in the middle of the double bed. Lately he had been sleeping with his back to me, or a little away from me, to protect his tender abdomen from any pressure. That night, adjusting to fit after each turning, we were more than usually close together, the full length of our bodies, and I was half-conscious of this all night long. Perhaps Wert knew, as I did not, that it was to be the last of the many nights we slept thus. His body never healed again sufficiently in the course of his mortal illness. I knew only, as he slept, that he was at deep, warm peace with himself and with me.

3

I prolonged my twenties, cut short my thirties, had in full my forties, and missed my fifties. It was a life rich in pleasure, and in the joy that goes deep; it was not lacking in the reverse of these, in sharp pain and bitter remorse; where it fell short was in accomplishment. I gambled with a career, not caring much for public acclaim, hoping for time to do the work that would give me satisfaction in good work, but always ready to postpone the effort for the sake of experience (which I always thought would enrich the work) or even for transient pleasures. So I wasted time and squandered vitality (of which I seemed to have plenty) and at forty-seven, when I put the career first, I needed perhaps fifteen years to make one. I got half of them, and it is useless to speculate on how good the work might have been if I had had the other half. I wasn't a born artist, a born novelist, or a born anything else. I had a talent for writing. I was working toward a clarity of communication, often at the expense of good writing; my last book, which tried to communicate more, had more glaring faults than anything I had written;

it was almost the book of an amateur writer. Could I have made myself an artist in another seven or eight years? I don't know. It doesn't matter. I wish I had written a better book than *The Death of Kings* if only so that *The Death of Kings* would be remembered. But it is a wish without deep regret. I was never an artist as a writer, but I was a little bit of an artist in knowing how to live. And what would be the satisfaction of knowing yourself an artist if you couldn't feel yourself a man?

This was a separate note I found on the long, yellow pages, a summing-up.

It would be inexcusable to prettify a portrait of this man. He liked being himself and was kind to himself in the way that made it easy to like him and feel kindly about him unless you hated him. He was clear and tough-minded about his faults, which he came to accept but never to admire. Other men might survive with integrity maimings, long imprisonment, mental illness, being deaf, blind, or bedridden, and still contribute value to life. Wert was a bad compromiser. He continually sought, with discipline, insight, and vitality, a delicate balance of all his forces that led continually up to his moments of intense fulfillment. When he was in control of his life, he gave more to other people by being as he was than anyone I ever knew. When he was forced to fight for this control, when the imbalance was too pronounced, he could be cruel, ungenerous, mean. He had determined, in his mid-forties, never again to allow himself to be caught in a position where he would behave in ways which he despised. His limitations defined, he would discipline circumstances so that his strengths might be tested, but his weaknesses protected. When he was sick, he barricaded himself indignantly against the effects on him of illness or bed. Sometimes he did it with drink, sometimes with humor and hypochondriacal flights of fancy which we called Wertenbaker's Medical Theories. When he was really sick, he was unreasonable, self-disgusted, cantankerous, and sometimes absurd.

I remember when he had scarlet fever. He not only got up and went to a bullfight in the rain, he also took a whole bottle of ten-year-old pills a doctor had once given him for flu. "They're supposed to cure me," he growled.

It was a measure of his uneasiness now that he was ready to leave for the train in the morning in more than an absolute minimum of time to catch it. An impatient man anyway, Wert felt there was no point to prolonging a respite. We sat in the living room near the fire which had been lit for him to breakfast beside, waiting for Dominique Toyos, a fisherman, neighbor, and friend, whose son, Begnat, was Chris's best friend. Dominique would put us aboard the train in Bayonne and return the car to the house. It was another sunny day, but it had turned very cold in the night.

Chris came into the room in his positive way, carrying his guitar in its battered case. He had put a scarf around his neck in deference to the sharp change in temperature, but his bare legs stuck a very long way out of short French pants. Ama was protesting from the kitchen that he should change to trousers, but once dressed for the day it took a major skirmish to make Chris change. He said, "Bawwwww," the local expression of indifference, and closed the door. Chris and his father regarded each other amiably. They were very much alike, with the same interior discipline and the same irritable dislike of outside interference in their lives. They even got up exactly the same way and were both speechless until well after breakfast. They had the same grins and matching humorousness, the same decisiveness, eagerness about living and learning, and the rare ability to be pleased with it if they got what they wanted. Both sybarites and demanding of others, they sometimes clashed with violence and when they did Wert won. Chris accepted this with pride, albeit not graciously. Already Chris as well as his father demanded a great deal from himself. They understood each other profoundly.

" 'Bye, Pop," said Chris. He hesitated, put down his guitar, and went over and shook hands with Wert, then kissed him hastily on both cheeks, French style, picked up his guitar and went out, banging the door, off to his rehearsal with the guitar and mandolin orchestra, the *Estudiantina de Ciboure*.

Wert, who had made no move to underline this parting, said, "Fine boy, our son."

Timberlake wandered into the room, approached her father by the most circuitous route, as she did when angling for a game of roughhouse with him, then leaned into him with great gentleness, nuzzling his cheek while he patted her rump. She was going to Baba's, she said, to play, and would Pop please toot the horn when he passed so she could wave goodbye.

Wert, whose relations with his daughter were warm and mystified, pinched her knee lightly as a token of games to come when he was feeling strong again, and sent her off. *"Charnelle,"* Wert said, since there was no delicate equivalent word in English.

The trip is vivid to me, in takes. I see Wert, looking very well, with his enviable dark sunburn for so late in the season, in the dark brown rough tweed jacket that particularly became him, a brindle Mexican tie with a railroad pattern, in discreetly gay colors, running upside down its length, with a green handkerchief that blended the light green shirt and the green-tinted prescription sun glasses he wore. Before packing them, he had used his fine, worn accouterments—the Rolls razor, the eighteenth-century mustache scissors from Hermès. He tended himself well, taking his time and pleasure in all the details of this. If I dwell a little, now, on the physical side of his pride, it is partly because I believe that men lose something when they do not preen their male feathers.

The compartments on the train were crowded and ours included a middle-aged Frenchwoman with two children returning to Paris for the October opening of the schools. She fed them continually out of an immense package of cheese, sausages, fruit, bread, and bonbons, but they were still restless and scrambled from door to window, with polite apologies when they stepped on our feet.

The train, the Sud-Express, ran fast and smokelessly through the familiar changes of landscape: flat pine country south of Bordeaux, which reminded me of my Alabama South; the rolling rich Dordogne, which reminded Wert of parts of his Virginia; the gray towns of Angoulême and Poitiers, which were historically interesting but until recently had had no hotels as comfortable as the country inns between; the Loire River which divided France, both in territory and character, into its north and its south; Tours, where we always celebrated this universal national division by stopping for a bottle of Vouvray no matter what time of day it was.

We took as long as possible over the pleasant lunch served in the *wagon-restaurant,* over a half-bottle of the French railroad's special *Château-Neuf-du-Pape.* Following the sensible French convention that good food tastes better if you talk about food while eating, we spoke of this one and of other meals we had eaten. Bordeaux, where the train stopped for fifteen minutes, was a favorite town of ours to eat in, and the Dubern was a favorite restaurant. Bordeaux no longer rates as a gourmet's town, but the headwaiter at Dubern gave his attention to seeing that we had food commensurate with the great bottles of Bordeaux red that had lain so long untouched in their cellars and that could be drunk there older than almost anywhere else.

Back in the compartment we were constrained by their

presence, although our companions were not English-speaking. Wert could not say the urgent thing he was thinking. We talked a little, sporadically, more for the relaxation of this than for entertainment, more to cue in our parallel thoughts than to express them.

Landmarks endlessly reminded us of other trips through France. It is such an agreeable country to travel in, especially by car as we usually did: the well-tended, well-loved earth; the beautiful if unspectacular countryside, always a different countryside, subtly changing color, architecture, contour, and form within a few hours' drive; the good roads protected against billboards by law; the innumerable pleasant places to stay. Ciboure to Paris was a comfortable day and a half for us in a small car, but we had once taken five days for it, zigzagging from restaurant to restaurant, eating more hours than we drove, arriving with indigestion—the worthwhile, well-earned kind of indigestion.

The changing light of the afternoon and the change toward fall as we moved directly north made color the key to memory. For pure color, seasonless, infinitely shaded to immense horizons, there was Spain, with its reds over browns; for greens there was the sweetly dying earth of Wert's Virginia; for yellows over grays there was West Texas; for purples and pinks, Italy; for the most flamboyant natural reds, New Mexico.

All the places we had been to, visited, revisited, lived in together, or known separately, belonged to us both, in spite of our different ways of remembering and incorporating them, of sharing and resharing them. Between us, our territorial coverage was extensive. I had been in Japan, Korea, Manchuria, and across Russia, which he had not. He knew Central and South America, Canada, Finland, Tunisia, which I did not. But we had been most fortunate because all we loved best we had shared most completely. Our natal South we had gone back into together, after our marriage. In 1950, we had bought a 1928 Rolls Royce and put into it our two children and most of our personal property, including three typewriters, and had taken a wide look at our native land, from New York to California. We had made, then furnished, then tended, a home of our own in Sneden's Landing beside the wide, fine, useful Hudson River. Before that, we had lived and worked in New York City, London, and Paris. We had chosen a village in the Basque country, Ciboure, in which to write, and from there all France, Spain, and Italy were easy to reach by car. On this trip, now, which was by the shortest and fastest route in order to reach not so much a destination as a destiny, we were both thinking of the accidental inspirations for, and the leisure of, so much of our former traveling.

Half-sentences were enough to recreate whole conversations between us—we'd been married so long and said so much. We did not talk much, now. Wert was gathering fatigue from weakness during the eight hours the train took to reach Paris.

Irwin's solid silhouette detached itself almost immediately from the crowd on the quai at the Gare d'Austerlitz. Marion Shaw and Barbara and Joe Kaufman were waiting outside the barrier. The faces of your friends are beautiful things to look upon, looking from your need to their concern, in such moments.

For seven years, since Wert had quit corporate work to do his own, we had closely rationed our social life—for reasons of economy, for fear of distraction from writing, because we found many social forms unrewarding, from laziness, in self-containment. We had seen much less of friends than before. Those who cared enough to do so understood that this was not because we had devalued them. They were rallying now, the four of them who knew we were in trouble.

The two women made a pool of glamour in the cold gray station, under whose roof it seemed to rain when it was raining outside, where angry, bundled-up and overloaded people were scrapping for porters and pushing to get into a queue for cabs, in the rain. Marion's Paris-pink curls glimmered and Barbara's dead-black polished cap of hair gleamed in the neon-broken squalid dark. Yet almost anyone could see that their shining good looks and chic were blurred and made imperfect by gentleness.

Joe Kaufman said: "We told Marion and Irwin not to break their dinner date. We're taking you to dinner." His manner was anxious and obdurate, which was the way he offered his wholly unreserved hospitality.

Barbara spoke to me alone as soon as she could. "Joe can't talk about it," she said, "but you know how he feels about Wert! Please promise me, *promise* me, Lael, you'll ask us for anything if you need it."

I think I sounded most reassuring when I told them what the physicians had given me to understand. Wert was benign about this. It was no part of his demands on people who loved him that they should worry about him or with him. I was also reassuring myself, which was different, and he was patient about this through dinner and until we were at last aboard the plane.

Wert had offered me the choice of saving our money, continuing my work, and staying with our children, instead of coming with him to share what could only be at best a distressing piece of time. We were both not only poor patients, but worse companions to the sick, shamed by illness, affronted by the body's departures from the normal healthy functionings in which we both took pleasure. It had been a free choice for me, freely offered. The reasons for deciding otherwise were perhaps the better reasons, but my decision had been whole in the instant of choice. There had been no hesitation, either, during the war, when I had left nine-month-old Chris behind with my mother because I could join Wert in England before the invasion.

Interdependence has its price. Wert would not let the choice, once I had made it, be a lesser one. I was feeling reassured and he was not, and this was also a form of separation.

As soon as we had unbuckled our seat belts and lit cigarettes in the air, he said the urgent thing which was on his mind: "If they open me up and find out the octopus is more extensive than it looked in the X rays, don't let them mess me up. Let me die on the operating table, that's all right, but *don't* let them make a mess of me."

We sat alone and the noise of the plane walled us in privacy. "It's *your* choice," I said, shaken and somber.

"Of course it is. But they won't let me make it. It'll be up to you if anyone. And don't you weaken. You hear me?"

"I hear you," I said. "Hear you and heed you."

"I trust you," he said.

I hoped he could, flinching. Now that we were this far on the way, and he had said what he had been waiting to say, fear and weariness hit me hard, together.

There was plenty of room, as we were on a plane that had been added to the schedule to take up an overflow. We could each have a section of three places, which meant we could stretch out and Wert could sleep. I can sleep over my paws, like a squirrel, but Wert had to be lying down. Deeply exhausted, he was now ready to sleep but not sure he could. He despised sleeping pills and would never take them. Bourbon whiskey was, he said, the proper gentleman's soporific. Since he wound up during the day rather than winding down, a matter that had required considerable adjustment between us since I did the opposite, he needed his bedtime highballs to relax. "There'll be time enough for sobriety in the damned hospital," he said, and decided to risk the discomfort whiskey might cause him now. He could always delight me when he chose to, turn any mood, or keep me up.

When we reached Shannon airport two hours later, we bundled up and slithered out into the freezing rain to go inside. When we sat down at a table to order cups of tea, an elderly gentleman, who proved to be in the diplomatic service, came up to us.

"Do you mind if I join you?" he asked wistfully. "You seem to be having such a very good time."

Afterwards we did sleep, a while, as the plane moved on into the dawn that came five hours sooner and thirty degrees hotter than it should have.

4

The raging vitality of the northeastern United States always affected us both immediately, coming to it first as we had from the South, returning to it as we did from Europe.

"Ohwhataviolentcountry," said Wert, making a refrain of it. It was thus he repeated "Ohwhatabeautifulcity" each time Paris struck him afresh. He had theories about the effect of the soil of places on the people who cultivated it, built upon it, ate its products. "If you don't cut our grass in Ciboure," he remarked once, "it gets ragged and you feel reproached for neglecting it, for being an uncivilized landlord. If you don't cut our grass at Sneden's Landing, it goes straight back to flourishing weeds in a month, to jungle in a year. Americans are in a battle with nature to be civilized at all."

There was a heat-and-humidity wave overwhelming the city of New York on that October 1st when we landed. We had not been in heat like that since New York, August, 1951. There wasn't any heat like that in France. I liked it, liking heat, and also the feeling of being immediately where I was, that it could be no other place in the world. Wert liked to make all changes at his leisure, with time for consideration, to travel across oceans by slow boat, to adjust himself minutely and consciously to each difference that places offered. There had been no time, even for thinking behind and ahead. This was not the homecoming to live there we had planned for 1956, when Chris would be thirteen. This was a temporary displacement-by-violence of our lives. Wert treated it as such, reacting as I have often seen soldiers do in war, with a kind of withdrawal that exposed as little as possible of himself to his environment. He neither complained of the heat nor the drag of his winter overcoat on the unaccustomed weakness of his arm nor commented on the smoke-muted, sun-shimmering skyline of the city as we approached it.

"Did Jim say he'd be there when we got there?" he asked me, referring to the telephone call I had made at the airport to Dr. Danielson's uptown office.

"No. I gather you'll be installed, X rays checked, records taken, all that, and Jim'll be at the hospital this afternoon around five."

Reminding me again of wartime attitudes, Wert shrugged, tolerant-intolerant at the prospect of tedium between climaxes to come.

The enormous, middle-aged hospital of which Jim was chief surgeon had entrances on two avenues and two streets in Manhattan. It was in a district where the modifying color was the more-brown-than-white of the Mexican and Puerto Rican peoples. The numerous signs were in both English and Spanish. As hospitals went, we approved of it. It had no chic, was neither cheerful nor drab, exuded no odor of charity nor of sanctity, seemed no more a world-of-its-own than any other busy corporation. Wert's place in it had already been established by his illness and certified by his doctor.

While we waited downstairs in a warren of offices for the forms of admission to be okayed, Wert annoyed himself by reading the booklet of hospital rules. He glowered when he came to the one strictly limiting all visitors to certain hours, looked over at me, and then, remembering, as I did, hundreds of instances when we, respecting the principles behind the rules, had broken rules, military, institutional, and social, he grinned. There are techniques for breaking rules, in contradistinction to fighting them, and we were practiced.

Upstairs in a wing reserved for major surgical cases, a

young doe-eyed resident physician named Dr. Martinez took the preliminary case history and made the examination, for which Wert was asked to undress and go to bed. The resident was a recent citizen and spoke English with an accent. His attitudes were Spanish. He granted such a man as Wert the respect and courtesy of explicit answers to questions he need not and should not have asked if he did not want the answers. Martinez understood fortitude as a virtue distinct from courage. It was certainly cancer, the growth. The X rays were first-rate. The cancer appeared small and "ideally" placed for complete removal. A considerable footage of intestines would be taken out to guard against recurrence. Wert was lucky that it was on the right side and not on the left. Operating on the left meant closing off the rectum and the patient eliminated into a bag for the rest of his life. Cancer on the left was the most painful of cancer's many forms because it squeezed the intestines closed. Recovery from an extensive operation on the right was grim enough, while the foreshortened intestinal system was readjusting, but a successful operation meant complete recovery. Martinez drew pictures on a prescription pad to illustrate the operation Dr. Danielson would, in his opinion, perform. Until the surgeon got inside, he added simply, there was no way in the world to be sure about metastasis—and not even then.

As was expected of me in the United States, I had gone out during the examination. The waiting room at the end of the hall was set about with maple furniture covered in chintz. The magazines, which had been more thumbed than read, were out of date. I eyed the telephone booth and remembered that I had not yet acquired a nickel and then that one nickel was no longer sufficient for a telephone call. Besides, there was a telephone installed in the room Jim had assigned to Wert. A man with a face like a walnut sat down opposite me, holding a modified sombrero on his knees. We exchanged nods and he adopted a diffident half-smile which I could either ignore or respond to, letting him talk. He told me, with a Texas accent, that his wife was there with a heart attack. This was the one malady of our day that killed more people than cancer, but I knew that if I mentioned the word cancer he would shrivel, his dread and sympathy making any relations with me, an amiable stranger, impossible. I should have carried a bell warning that I was conversationally unclean, out-of-bounds. I found out later that the *Herald Tribune* still did not admit to cancer as a cause of death in its obituaries.

I wandered along the corridor to make sure I was not outwaiting the resident, and saw Wert's room door open to catch what air could be coaxed through from stifling street to stifling hall. When I hesitated at the door, the two gentlemen cordially invited me in. Wert, no longer the medically interviewed, but the interviewer, was looking refreshed. His much-laundered thin white silk pajamas matched the young doctor's starched much-laundered white coat. They had the air of being cool and friendly together.

"Your husband asked me more questions than I asked him," said Dr. Martinez, delighted.

"I hope you satisfied his curiosity," I said. "That's one reason we came home. Our French collapses in emergencies."

"I prefer Spaniards anyway," said Wert.

He was referring to their offhand attitude toward death, their recognition that no matter how often he is reprieved every man must die. When Wert had been found in a ditch under his overturned car after hitting a tree on the road between Zaragoza and Barcelona in 1927, peasants had piled him into a hayload and driven him to the nearest village. Wert came to long enough to demand that they telephone Zaragoza for an ambulance to take him on to Barcelona and then relapsed into unconsciousness. When he came to again it was in the ambulance en route back to Zaragoza. He insisted on being taken instead to Barcelona. "You're going to die anyway," said the attendant, "so that's silly. Zaragoza is a very nice place to die." Wert maintained that he preferred

Barcelona. The argument remained on the plane of which was the better town to die in. Wert got them turned around. A little later a personal need became urgent. He insisted that they stop the ambulance. "You'll die right now if you get up," said the attendant cheerfully. Wert replied that it was his business. The driver and the attendant agreed to this. Staggering to his feet in spite of a couple of broken ribs, a busted cheekbone, concussion, and whatever else, he relieved himself out the rear door of the ambulance. It was back in the middle of the same village and a crowd gathered around. Everybody cheered. "Maybe the señor will not die," said the attendant, more admiring than pleased. We spent a lot of time in 1948 on that same road looking for the tree and the village in commemoration of his survival and his immense enjoyment of the scene, until Wert identified many trees and several villages as "the one" and the search became a joke.

Wert began to show me the drawings of intestines Martinez had made for his benefit and then desisted, recognizing the squeamishness I tried to hide.

"I'm a sissy," I said apologetically, wishing that I were not. I still turned my head away, like a fool, at the sight of a hypodermic needle and had to steel myself to take care of the children competently when they injured themselves or were sick. Nurses I thought wonderful and nerveless.

Another young resident doctor came in, a Virginian. He asked if by any chance it was—and it was indeed, coincidentally—Wert's father who had delivered the young man into the world the year before Dr. Wertenbaker had died of cancer.

So we talked of Virginia. Of Spain. Exchanged jokes. Both residents laughed gleefully over Wert's description of the morning his father had shown him his film—one of the first medical films for use in teaching, which Dr. Wertenbaker had made—of various ways to deliver babies. Wert had asked to see it, and the doctor had chosen the morning to satisfy his son's curiosity when Wert had a monumental bourbon hangover. Each sequence began with a well-focused closeup of the female area involved. "Nearly turned me against women, bourbon, and babies," said Wert.

How much did these two actually give for Wert's chances at that moment? I don't know.

The Virginian told a story, I remember, of a charity patient who drank too much and had stomach-aches. His family, Italians, had dragged him protesting to the hospital. Ordinary tests and X rays showed nothing. In the normal course of things he'd have been discharged on a diet with a vague diagnosis of gastroenteritis. But at that moment they wanted a subject for "the works," including an exploratory operation, for demonstration purposes. Here was a charity patient about whose condition there was an area of vague doubt. The "poor bugger" turned out to have a cancer too small to be found otherwise. "We might well have been causing the guy a lot of unnecessary misery. As it was, we probably saved his life." This story entered Wert's and my conversations about the fantasies of fortune later on.

I know the doctors were enjoying Wert, taking a rare half hour out of their overburdened schedules to enjoy him. They did not temper their talk to our supposed limitations as patient and lady. I was reminded again of wartime.

When Dr. James Danielson came into the room, the young men snapped to deferent attention. Medical service is strict, almost military, about rank and protocol.

Jim is a very big man, six-foot-three or more, and hefty, although not fat. He has a benign, plain face, the ponderous, profound gentleness that can go with unusual size in men or dogs, and a slow-speaking deep voice. He moves slowly and uprightly, making very certain gestures and no nervous ones. In the eight years since I had seen him last he had grayed from his temples through his hair. I had known him twenty-two years. When I had first met him, his air of medical authority, reinforced by his size, was still a young man's deliberate performance and you knew that he had come from the country and would make good in New York. Now his assurance seemed real and almost as if he no longer questioned his own vulnerability, his human liability to error. In so far as this was true, I believed it based on the confidence that conservative, painstaking, and superior craftsmen come honestly to place in themselves. An artisan, proud of his ability and his trade, an honest man, Jim was what we needed now. Nor had he gotten where he was, chief surgeon of this hospital, consultant at another more important one, head of an enormous military hospital during the war, on anything but ability and the respect of his profession. Besides, Wert liked him and considered him a man.

The operation was scheduled for Tuesday. This would allow time to stuff Wert with antibiotics to ward off postoperative complications. Jim would operate at 8:30 A.M. Wert made a face at this and Jim laughed.

"See you tomorrow . . ." Jim and the two residents went out.

"Well, I guess I'm in pretty good hands," said Wert. The rueful undertone derived from his dislike of being in any hands but his own.

"I'll call Suzie and then remove that thing from your sight," I said, indicating the telephone.

The telephone was Wert's particular *petite bête noire*. Once freed of the necessity for using it in business, he had spoken into it only once in seven years. I had served as intermediary when people called him, as if I were a translator interpreting from a mechanical to a living language. Our telephone at Sneden's Landing was in the kitchen and the buzzer was so light he could not hear it elsewhere. He maintained it wasted time, interfered intolerably with all forms of concentration, and that its bland, blind interruptions of life were exceedingly bad for you. He did not mind it so much in France, where it was still treated, on the whole, as an instrument for grave and minimum use—in the country, that is.

"It unplugs," he said. "Keep it. Unplug it. Plug it in and use it when you want to."

"You're getting soft," I said.

Suzie's vibrant, well-articulated voice sprang along the wire.

"I was *just* sitting down to cable you that Gleaves and I were coming to stay with you in Ciboure after our trip to England," she said. "What lousy timing. *Of course* you have a bed here. Will that man let me speak to him or won't he?"

He would, to my surprise.

"Oh that voice!" said Suzie, after Wert handed the telephone back to me.

I began to unpack the rest of the things Wert would need in the hospital and to repack his suitcase to take along with mine to Suzie's.

"Don't set up housekeeping in here too thoroughly," said Wert. "I'd like, if it's all right with you, to stay here until Tuesday in solitary peace, but after that I'd better go into a multi-bed room. Our insurance doesn't cover a single."

"Let's think about that tomorrow," I said. We were both drained and wanted to get settled, comfortable, to talk a bit quietly.

Wert dressed, shaky as he was feeling.

When the first nurse came in, she found me installed on top of the bed and Wert sitting in the armchair.

"Well, well," she exclaimed in a high-pitched, well-meaning, nursery-school voice. "But remember Dr. Danielson says you are not to leave the hospital, Mr. Winterbacher. Here's your cocktail . . ." She handed Wert a revolting mixture of oil and milk of magnesia in a paper cup.

A brisk, pretty nurse came in with eight capsules of whatever mycin it was that the first nurse had forgotten. "You'll

42

have to get down a lot of these before Tuesday," she said, "sir."

Wert took the capsules in the palm of one hand, the paper cup in the other, threw all the capsules back toward his tonsils, and followed them with the "cocktail."

"That's one way of doing it," said the pretty nurse.

"Anything's better than swallowing eight pills one at a time," said Wert. " 'You cain't do that!' "

"He's a card, isn't he?" said the first nurse.

They went out and Wert said, "Get me some cracked ice, for the Lord's sake, and please see that *Numero Uno* doesn't get in here again. I can take cutie-pie."

Jim had said Wert was welcome to have a few drinks over the weekend. The drugstore across the street from the hospital yielded me a container of cracked ice, a lemon as a favor, some honey, soda, an all-purpose Scout knife, the daily papers, my brand of cigarettes—Wert had brought his black French favorites in cartons—free matches, two ash trays, a paper-back Shakespeare's tragedies, a Yardley's shaving bowl, gumdrops and mints, a folder of Sight-savers for wiping reading glasses, a "Slinky," which I could not resist, pencils with erasers on the end, a long yellow pad of ruled paper, tooth powder, as only paste was sold in Ciboure, and some cheese and crackers for canapés. Someone has remarked that if the Germans or the Russians ever invaded America, they would never get past the first drugstore.

The narrow little room with its beige walls, severe bureau and one straight chair, enameled hospital bed and side table, and maple easy chair with flat, hard arms which we had placed in social juxtaposition to the bed, was suffused with a smoky, rosy light from the sunset when I got back. Wert watched, approving, while I made him an old-fashioned to his particular specifications: dollop of dark honey, tablespoon of tepid water to dissolve it in, cracked ice to the top of the glass, sour-mash bourbon poured over the ice, fine spray from

43

the twisted lemon peel evenly distributed over the top, peel rubbed around rim of glass, then dropped in drink, whole handled with care so that fingers touched only the bottom of the glass.

The anywhere time of the evening ended with a blaze of ceiling light and a dinner tray for Wert.

"Don't watch me eat this slop," said Wert, regarding the mashed potatoes and the string beans and the overdone meat. "Go do what you have to and come back. Unless you're too tired."

"I'll be back. Do you want to see anybody at all over the weekend?" I asked, thinking the time might be enlivened by a few very special friends, knowing how much the Gleaveses would want to see him.

Wert expressed the opinion that a hospital was no goddamned place to see anybody in, no goddamned place to be, and that he'd be goddamned glad to see the last of it, even feet first.

It was impossible to think at that moment that he had anything more than a minor illness. When Suzie and Charlie asked, all affection and anxiety, how he was, I said that he was very much himself.

There are no notes in Wert's *carnet* on the pages for October 2nd, 3rd and 4th. We took our ease, Southern fashion, in the heat like Southern summer heat, in the room Wert left only for his daily showers down the hall. As we exchanged bed for armchair at intervals, talked or did not, through the slow days and nights, lingering together until midnight, we might have been exchanging hammock for lawn chair, on a wide porch, or under pine trees. Our Southernness was not dominant in either of us, but we could both rock away time that had no better purpose.

Wert had planned to make a few notes on his projected new novel—the one his editor and agent were so excited over and for which the publishing house had offered the week before a very satisfactory advance on nothing more than the

44

outline—but he did not. His working mind was, he said, in abeyance, and anything he did would only be to do over. So the yellow pad and the jackknife-sharpened pencils stayed in the drawer. The books he had chosen were piled tidily on the table. He read only the *Selected Montaigne,* finding it suited his random thinking. There were no flowers in the room, since he was subject to hay fever, and no photographs, since he claimed they interfered with his mental images.

Still, we did not want to change the bare room that had become ours for any other. Jim aided me by saying that if Wert was an unsociable man, a mild enough description of Wert when sick, it would be a more than justifiable extravagance to keep him alone.

Anything Wert said then about his mortality or his mortal concern for his children was later said better. Antibiotics depressed him and he was very conscious of the artificiality of such depression. He inclined to discuss the practical and was cautious of either antic or philosophic thoughts, testing what he intended to say for the flat sound of strings gone slack. His was a critical ear for the music as well as the words of speech. Besides, he was afraid, and afraid of the influence of fear as well as that of medicine. His fear was not of the verdicts of fate in the future but that he might accept those verdicts on anything less than his own best terms.

"Don't you let me let myself down!" he demanded once.

His preferences in terms of his fate he laid down precisely and in order to Jim and to me.

One:

" 'Is Life Worth Living? This is a question for an embryo, not for a man.' Samuel Butler, 1883." He quoted the old iconoclast with whom he enjoyed agreeing and disagreeing. Life being well worth living, he would live if he could, if there was reason to suppose he might survive from however unpleasant an operation into excellent if not youthful health. "I'll take my fifties on reasonable terms if I get them," he said.

Two:

He would settle for a piece of good time, however limited, if it was *good* time. The past year had been good time, superior time, in spite of the cancer manifesting itself in his intestines. He would take his disease and the inevitable progression and end thereof rather than submit to drastic remedies therefor.

Three:

If the surgeon did not operate within the limits already defined, or let him alone, he would please let him die. Would I kindly persuade our medical man that the patient's third choice was to die on Tuesday? There was no fourth choice.

What he rejected, growing irascible at the thought of how often this was made possible in our age of medical miracles, was to live on crippled and incomplete, learning the ways and demands of living at any price, dependent on others, being less than himself, less than a whole man.

The possibility of recurrence, after the most successful operation, was detestable, but not a present problem. That kind of fear was not his kind of fear. Wert had never played for security in his life.

"Your guy is a tough man to deal with," said Jim, during our private interview in his office on Monday in the early afternoon. "Lael, if it has metastasized to the left . . ."

"You do only what he tells you you're to do!" I said.

"People often change their minds," said Jim gently, "when it comes right down to it. No matter how they talk. You learn to live with a lot of things. It's better than dying, you know."

If I had wavered then, from one simple premise as the wife of a grown man, I would have destroyed the best that came later, to no purpose. There were many reasons for wavering at this moment, better ones than for not, if you like. Wert could change his mind. He had already once during this affair. The word of next-of-kin is often the deciding one. I might be literally condemning my beloved if I were intransigent.

"Be reasonable, Lael," said Jim, convincing and kind.

Arguments with Wert occurred to me, mostly old ones. They seemed fairly persuasive away from any testy rebuttals of his. We, Wert and I, went over this complex time of temptation later. If I had yielded, ever so little, I would either have veiled it from Wert or told him about it, and in either case he would have known it, and understood that it was for love of him. His love for me would not have been affected, only the quality of his trust, which would have changed everything. It was not easy to stick to that single premise in the face of the responsibility Jim was handing me. It was not a question of the honor of my word to Wert. It was more basic than that. Even if life might be at stake, Wert was fifty-three years old and he had not given me the responsibility for any decision concerning him. He had kept that responsibility for himself.

"Damn it," I said, "he's the boss."

Jim lifted his big hands and then resettled them on his desk. He talked a little about the operation that he expected and hoped to perform in the morning, on the right side. It would be fifteen days before Wert could leave the hospital. After that, he asked, did I have somewhere to take Wert to convalesce before we returned to Europe? I had. Suzie and Charlie had offered us their house while they were away, and as much room in it as we needed when they returned.

Cheerfully, and with only a most conventional-sounding warning to the effect that in these cases nothing was entirely certain, Jim sent me off.

Later in the day, on his final pre-operative visit to Wert at the hospital, Jim told him that I was a very stubborn lady. He added, according to Wert, that he would be gratified to think his wife had as complete confidence in *him*.

This evening was a little different from Friday, Saturday

and Sunday. Wert was given little to eat and would be put to sleep with a shot at ten-thirty. I called John and Frances Ann Hersey in Connecticut on the telephone. They were too close to us not to be told until the operation was over. I promised to call them as soon as it was over the next day. Wert said to tell them to save the champagne and *don't* send flowers. Just before I left the hospital, Wert pointed out a marker in the *Selected Montaigne*.

"I want you to read that while I'm downstairs tomorrow," he said. "The essay 'That Men Are Not to Judge of Our Happiness Till after Death.' What a title!"

We said good night, knowing that nothing separated us.

"I am a very happy man," said Wert.

5

Till man's last day is come, we should not dare
Of happiness to say what was his share;
Since of no man can it be truly said
That he is happy till he first be dead.
(OVID, Metamorphoses)

Children know the story of King Croesus, to this effect,
that, having been taken prisoner by Cyrus and condemned
to die, as he was about to be executed he cried out, "O
Solon! Solon!" This being reported to Cyrus, and he in-
quiring what it meant, Croesus gave him to understand
that he was now verifying at his own expense the warning
Solon had once given him, namely, that men, however
Fortune may smile upon them, cannot be called happy
until they have been seen to pass the last day of their lives,
because of the uncertainty and mutability of human
things, which at a very slight impulse change from one
state into another, entirely different. And for this reason
Agesilaus replied to someone who was saying that the
King of Persia was happy to have come so young to so
mighty a kingdom: "True, but neither was Priam un-
happy at that age." In a short space of time kings of Mace-
don, successors to the mighty Alexander, are turned into
carpenters and clerks at Rome; tyrants of Sicily, into
schoolmasters at Corinth. A conqueror of one half of the
world and chief of so many armies is turned into a miser-

able suppliant to the rascally officers of a king of Egypt: such was the cost to the great Pompey of having his life prolonged five or six months. And in our fathers' days, Lodovico Sforza, the tenth duke of Milan, under whom all Italy had so long trembled, was seen to die a prisoner at Loches, but not till he had lived ten years there, which was the worst part of his fortune. The fairest of queens,* widow of the greatest king in Christendom, has she not just died by the hand of an executioner? And a thousand such examples. For it seems that, as storms and tempests become angered at the pride and loftiness of our buildings, there are also spirits above that are envious of the grandeurs here below.

> *So much so does some hidden force o'erwhelm*
> *Human affairs, and is seen trampling on*
> *The glorious rods and axes powerful,*
> *Making a mockery of those stately signs.*
>
> (LUCRETIUS)

And it seems that Fortune sometimes lies in wait for precisely the last day of our lives to show her power to overthrow in a moment what she had been so many years in building, and she makes us cry out with Laberius: *Certainly I have this day lived one day more than I ought to have done.* (MACROBIUS, *Saturnales*)

In this sense the good advice of Solon may reasonably be taken. But since he is a philosopher, men for whom the favors and disgraces of Fortune rank neither as happiness nor unhappiness, and with whom grandeurs and power are accidents of an almost indifferent nature, I find it likely that he had some further aim, and that his meaning was that this very felicity of our life, which depends upon the tranquillity and contentment of a wellborn spirit and upon the resolution and assurance of a well-ordered soul, ought never to be attributed to any man

* Mary Queen of Scots.

until he has been seen to play the last, and doubtless the hardest, act of his comedy. There may be disguise in all the rest: either these fine philosophical discourses are only for the sake of appearance, or circumstances, not testing us to the quick, give us leisure to keep our countenance always calm. But in this last scene between death and ourselves there is no more counterfeiting; we must speak plain, we must show what there is good and clean in the bottom of the pot,

> *For then at last from deep within his breast*
> *True words are forced, the mask is wrenched away,*
> *Reality remains.*

> (LUCRETIUS)

That is why all the other actions of our life ought to be tried and tested by this last act. It is the master-day, it is the day that is judge of all the rest, "it is the day," says one of the ancients, "that must judge all my past years." To death do I refer the test of the fruit of all my studies. We shall then see whether my reasonings come only from my mouth or from my heart.

. . . .

There are brave and fortunate deaths. In the case of a certain man* I saw death cut the thread of a marvelously advancing progress, in the flower of its growth, with an end so lofty that, in my opinion, his ambitious and courageous designs contained nothing so high as was their interruption. He reached the place to which he aspired, without making his way to it, more grandly and gloriously than he could have hoped or desired. And he surpassed by his fall the power and name to which he aspired in his career.

In judging the life of another, I always observe how the end was borne; and one of the principal concerns of my

---

* Etienne de la Boétie; it has also been suggested that he may have had the Duc de Guise in mind.

own life is that the end be borne well, that is, calmly and insensibly.

—From MONTAIGNE, *Selected Essays*
Charles Cotton–W. Hazlitt translation

It had been a little after eight when they wheeled Wert off in his bed. He was calm and partially insensible. I believe he had been given a preanesthetic shot, but it was hard to tell about him in the early morning. We had exchanged a grip of hand and eyes, but said nothing to each other.

As soon as it opened at nine o'clock, I went down to the hospital coffee shop to get a container of coffee or Coke to drink in the room. The operation, in principle, was a long one. Jim would come up as soon as he could. This was time merely to be got through. As I sat on a stool waiting for my order, I saw a vivid couple push into the entrance hall through the revolving doors just beyond the coffee shop entrance. Before I saw their faces I knew them and cried out to them. It was John and Frances Ann Hersey. They had come in from Connecticut to be with me.

"We didn't say we were coming because you'd have told us not to come," said Frances Ann in her flat, warm voice.

"Dear Lael," said Johnny.

It had been many years since Wert and I had bothered to have friends as part of our lives who were too unequally the friends of one of us. There wasn't time. But there were small imbalances in most relationships, natural ones since we were not only male and female but very dissimilar people, Wert and I. With the Herseys the parts of friendship were in rare total balance. When we traveled together, in Mexico, in Spain, everything we did had an easy rhythm, made a kind of dance, accompanied by four-part conversational harmony. I think almost they alone could have moved so gracefully into the loneliness of that hour.

Johnny was carrying a bottle of Waterfill and Frazier

whiskey, a brand of bourbon we had drunk in Mexico on our first trip there together, a gay, fine trip. We called the partners who manufactured this brand "Doctor Frazier and Old Bladderfill" and nicknamed each other Jack, Chuck, Fanny and Lilly, laughing at ourselves for the simple-minded fun we were having. Frances Ann and I saw our first bullfight in Mexico City, terrified beforehand and both sure we would hate it for the blood and cruelty and thus would be unable to share a profound enthusiasm of both our husbands'. There are reasons, the most decent ones, for hating bullfights, and for liking them, and bad reasons for not liking them, and bad reasons for liking them. We liked them, for the same complicated reasons which we found good—after Frances Ann's and my first one, we all four did—and forgave ourselves for liking them in spite of the reasons for not, and particularly liked being together when we saw them, there, and later in Spain. (This is no matter for argument—you do or you don't.) The bottle was symbol of all the things including bullfights we had all four enjoyed together.

Heartily embraced, I lost a small scarf I was wearing and we went back to find it before going upstairs. It was a blood-red square of flimsy rayon, the kind everybody knotted around their necks in Pamplona, Spain, during the fiesta of San Fermín. I had worn it as a talisman. Wert and I had been to five fiestas of San Fermín, arriving on the July 7ths of 1947, '48 and '49, of 1953 and '54. In 1947 we had been the only Americans there, indeed, almost the only foreigners. In 1953 we had seen Ernest Hemingway and Mary there, spotting them across the curve of the bull ring and exclaiming how suitable it was to see "Papa" Hemingway in that setting. In 1954 some of the flood of American youngsters coming for the first time to visit the scene of *The Sun Also Rises* had mistaken Wert for Hemingway. This mistake derived not so much from a superficial resemblance as from the affectionate respect with which the local Spaniards treated Wert. At some time during each fiesta Wert had said to me, "You're a good gal at a fiesta." It was a different thing for a man to feel from his liking for a wife—especially at San Fermín, which is decidedly a male fiesta. To the Herseys it needed no explanation why this scarf was the talisman it was.

I don't know what time it was when Jim came. We had not been settled long, the Herseys and I, in the room. I felt, in immediate alarm, that it was too soon. There is a note in Wert's *carnet* that he saw clearly the face of a clock, downstairs in the recovery room to which they took patients from the operating theatre, at 11:05. He also registered that it was too soon for him to be conscious. Jim courteously motioned the Herseys to leave and then sat down and I sat down again, too, having come to my feet when he entered.

He said immediately, "Lael, I have bad news for you."

I don't know in what order he told me the details. He had opened Wert up, taken samples, and closed the incision. Wert would recover fairly quickly from this operation, but he would not recover from the disease. The cancer had reached the liver. It was all over the liver. The liver was not dispensable.

I remember the effort to breathe and I remember saying, "Well, that's that. Now—how long does he have? How much good time?"

In his unprotected concern and affection Jim blurted out his real guess: three months. Then he went on talking, sometimes answering a question as I tried to think what Wert would want me to ask. I remember once Jim started to make a gesture of passing his hand under his chin as if to lift it, as if to tell me to keep my chin up, and then halted the gesture. After he pronounced the sentence of death we were no longer in much communication—even before the argument began.

Talking as both friend and physician he said that even if we had not so strictly enjoined him he preferred to remove no organs in such a case as he found. By removing part of the cancerous intestines he might have prolonged Wert's life a

54

little, but he himself did not believe in prolonging life "at the price of suffering" when it could not possibly be saved. He did not think the cancer would metastasize to the left before the liver had—well, killed Wert. He did not believe Wert needed to suffer, he saw no virtue in unnecessary pain. He would provide us with all the pain-killing drugs we could possibly need for this purpose . . .

Jim went on talking, quietly, kindly.

He was saying that no doctor was God or even godlike. A doctor who pronounced an estimate of the time it would take for a disease to kill an individual was foolish. Patients had outlived many sentences of death. Wert, now, might easily have a year, more, of time, time perhaps as good as that prior to the operation. Cancer was particularly unpredictable. The laboratory reports would help determine the speed of the malignant growth. From the case history it seemed fairly slow-growing. But—he must admit—the operation itself, however carefully executed, did sometimes scatter living cancer cells about to establish new colonies. There were experiments being made with injections which slowed growth. But . . . At any rate, Wert would be spared the expense and pain of conventional treatments, deep X rays for instance, as useless.

We were spared the torture of false hope.

"Now," said Jim gently, "what shall we tell Wert?"

"Tell him the truth," I said.

"You can't," said Jim. "You can't take hope away from a human being."

"*Is* there any hope?" I asked him.

"No," said Jim.

If there had been even a chance of a miracle, Jim would have said, instead, to pray for one.

"Then," I said, "that's that."

Jim's big, benign face was very drawn and I felt pity for him. "Have you ever seen anyone die?" he asked me.

"No," I said.

Madame Sueur's father had died of old age at ninety-seven. He was a superb old man when I first knew him, lazy, life-loving, and had never been sick a day in his life, or at least had never admitted to being. He had the perfectly round mask of a face pure Basques have when they do not have the long, bony-nosed faces they prefer to carve in wood. Old Man Gelos' body was in the square-shouldered, narrow-hipped, Egyptian-frieze style. At ninety-five he would climb springily up the hill from Kechiloa to Bordagain to see us. When he took to calling me "Mommy" instead of Madame, as did most of my middle-aged and youthful friends in Ciboure, it was considered a fine jest. During his last year he lost all of his faculties, miserably, slowly, one after the other. He accused his children of a conspiracy to kill him when the doctor refused to come any more because he could do nothing for a man who was dying of old age. Papa Gelos was very religious and very terrified of dying. There are better ways of dying than of old age. But I had not seen him actually die.

"I have," said Jim. "In my profession, many, many people. During the war—many courageous men who had proved their courage. Lael, I tell you, it is better if they hope. It is one thing to take a brave chance on dying and another to know that you are going to die—soon. You cannot take hope away from Wert."

"I cannot lie to this man," I said. "That would take his dignity away from him. He would rather have dignity than hope."

"You cannot know *any* man that well," said Jim.

"I know this man that well," I told him. Not through the brain or through love, but through sleeping in the same bed with him for more than four thousand nights. I knew him through the skin and I knew him that well.

"He may change," said Jim. People change, he told me, faced with death. He might get paranoid or suicidal. He might want to find quacks to tell him they could cure him. People clung to hope from any source, Jim said. Wert might, on the other hand, become very religious, saintly, turn to God . . .

I had half-smiled when Jim said Wert might take to quacks and now I think I smiled wholly and made an amused gesture of dismissal.

Jim said sharply, "He might! Would you try to stop him if he wanted to?"

"For the Lord's sake," I said, despairing of an understanding among us, reaching for one because it would mean a good deal to Wert if Jim would talk to him without reservations. "Wert's faiths are his own and they are strong ones. I think he will die by them. If he needs more, something else, to die by, I hope he has time to find, finds—God. It's his life and his death, not mine or yours, and you can't judge him for all you know. If he wants hope, I'll know it and give it to him, too. With all my heart. Lie my head off, if he changes and I feel him wanting me to. But I won't lie to him now. And he won't change."

You don't hear your own voice as you hear others', but there was a particular kind of rushing, echoing stillness in that room. Wert asked me to repeat our conversation two days later, as near word-perfect as I could. He was very curious about all this.

"You insist on telling him?" asked Jim.

"Yes," I said.

"I think you are wrong."

"I don't."

"When will you tell him?"

"As soon as he wants to know, which will be at once."

"I think you are wrong. Maybe you are cruel."

"*No!*"

That frightened me, though. No more was bearable at the moment, and Jim said, "Do you want to see your friends?"

I did, in a minute. Jim went out and in a minute the Herseys came in.

"Take your time," said Johnny softly.

Memory blurs at this point—I think only the things that affected Wert and me together stand out—except for the vise-like, brief hug Frances Ann gave me for courage out of love on the instant when they knew I was ready for them to go. I remember otherwise only saying, very nearly uncertain, "Of course I must tell Wert at once," and Johnny saying, with certainty, "Of course."

Charlie and Suzie Gleaves knew the morning's schedule, and my aunt and uncle who lived on Central Park West. These four, oldest friends and closest family, had fed and sheltered me, and concerned themselves deeply over the crisis. No one else knew even that we were on the continent, but these people were waiting at their telephones for news, since I had refused to let them be with me. After a while, during the interminable, timeless wait for Wert to come up, I called them. I believe I told Suzie then, and then realized that I could not say the words, definitive as they were, often. With Wert I had faced the theory that he might die, during the past week. More than two years before we had said to each other—on a walk up from the Peregordine along the Left Bank quais of Paris—"We've won!" *Hubris*—defiance of fate— feeling, saying, we'd had so much together that nothing could happen to us to make the total of our lives add up to less than fulfillment. We were vulnerable only through our children, who had good lives coming to them. But practice is not so simple as theory. My voice betrayed me to my sensitive and loving aunt, I think, although I only told her that it was "all right" and that I would come up there later.

When Wert was brought back to the room he looked wounded, beaten-up, drawn, and defiant. There was a tube up his nose that went into his stomach. The open end was taped to his forehead and resembled a periscope. He was obviously in pain. The nurse told me that the new system of bringing operative cases up to full consciousness immediately following an operation was most painful, but that it cut down postoperative complications.

"As soon as Doctor's seen him, we'll put him out cold again and keep him that way until tomorrow," she assured me.

Wert looked at me; his eyes wavered, and then focused hard. "Well?" he managed to say.

"It's—not—too—bad," I said. I was telling him he had his second choice. They had not messed him up. He had a piece of good time coming. But the sentence was death.

Wert nodded, understanding me exactly. He tried to smile and then his eyes went out of focus.

Jim came in and I left the room. By the time I was allowed back in, Wert was out, limp and deeply drugged.

There is a note in the *carnet* which reads: "News ex-Lael. (Knew it anyway.) Jim: 'We'll talk tomorrow.'"

6

Our marriage had survived all that it had to survive, including the high ideal we set for it from the first intensely romantic moments when we fell in love, at the ages of thirty-four and forty-two, in London, in wartime. By this I mean it survived deviations from the ideal and the ideal survived and we never settled down for less.

It survived wartime separations in wartime capitals and the first winter months in Ciboure when we saw no one else at all, before we had learned how to live that way. It survived an inexcusable and neurotic piece of behavior on my part in our second year of marriage; the seventy-six hours we went without sleep or an instant's separation violently settling with it; and the months when Wert continued to punish me after he had forgiven me and I continued to seek absolution after I had received it. It survived the year he took a job as an executive which he did not want and commuted to New York from its suburbs which he did not like and we spent too much money and lived badly and went into debt and he was at his sullenest and I was at my sloppiest. It survived a Little Toidey which I bought for Chris and Wert burned.

This last-mentioned incident was both comic and cosmic. All three of us lost our formidable tempers at once. I felt that I was defending women and children against the age-old tyranny of man and Wert felt that he was defending man against modern enslavement by women, children, and offensive gadgets. Chris was defending his selfish comfort in a universe still scaled too big for him. When the dust, or rather the ashes, of that battle settled, an enduring family peace was established, with Wert as undisputed head of his family. Later I got a china pot with roses on it for Chris, which Chris loved and his father admired. I found that the delight of yielding to a demanding man was great. I make no moral of this. You can only yield with such pride to a man whose respect for what he gets is as great as his desire to have it. I can only comment, in this short homily from a preacher's daughter, that a chain of command in a functioning unit of uncowed and contributing individuals operates better than a constant struggle for authority or what is sometimes called equality.

Wert made one note among many others for the book he was going to write called *The Time of Enchantment,* the middle book of the Barons trilogy, of which *The Barons* and *The Death of Kings* were the first and third volumes: "In all large organizations where one man is at the top, the others near the top will fight to get there, and so the morality of that organization will be conditioned by the struggle for power, and that morality will determine the organization's external, as well as its internal, dealings. The only way to avoid this power complex, this power struggle, is by keeping the organization small and powerless (as in a very small business or a very small kingdom) or by curbing the power of the top man by vesting power in other—and frequently hostile— organizations (as in checks and balances of U.S. government or kingship in Britain). Let loose the struggle for power anywhere, and it will destroy all other concepts."

In the small and powerless kingdom of our family, the amount of power retained in each pair of hands was early defined. This reduced considerably the turbulence generated by four positive personalities adjusting to each other within a succession of places and years and circumstances.

We were always at economic peace with each other, and

this is rarer than it sounds. I don't think Wert and I in twelve years ever had a quarrel based on money, who spent it for what, who made it or did not make it, and certainly not whose it was. When we married, I owned some clothes, household furnishings, and a typewriter. He had just paid off old debts, had a small amount of furniture, and five thousand dollars, with which we inexplicably bought land in Virginia, which we later inexplicably sold for no profit. We both had jobs. We found ourselves at the time in the middle-income middle class. Later we trespassed in the domain of the very, very rich on the unlimited expense accounts allowed by corporations to employees in wartime Europe. Later still we were dependent on our wildly fluctuating separate fortunes as writers. I always took a sensuous pleasure in being with Wert in luxurious surroundings. It was partly because he fitted so comfortably into them and, through luck or legerdemain, often managed to achieve them; it was partly for the feeling, derived from the proudly impecunious Southern heritage we shared, of trespassing where we claimed more right than many on whom we trespassed. This feeling was in no wise diminished by our disapproval, on the simplest principles, of the social bases of excessive luxuriousness. We were not solemn about it, but laughed at our own complacency. "Change your social status today, lady?" Wert asked me, as we dressed in our tourist cabin for dinner with first-class diplomatic friends on the S.S. America in 1952. "Are we rich or poor right now?" the children were apt to inquire before making a demand, without considering that the answer measured either our stability or our social standing. "They prided themselves," Wert wrote in his shelved and uncompleted novel about a married couple, "that they could move from ease to simplicity with simplicity and ease."

"Being reconstructed doesn't change us from being Southerners, and there's a lot we'll never have to explain to each other," Wert said, the second time we met. If it had not been for all that hadn't had to be explained, including a sense of physical integrity that had survived earlier casual relationships, and two previous marriages apiece, the hazards would have been greater. If it had not been for all that, I should have had more difficulty in understanding his conscience and his carelessness, his intolerance and his kindness, his silent moods and sudden joys, his perfectionism and his pleasure in getting drunk. He was a difficult man, but a most rewarding one.

"Tell it as a search . . ." and it was.

We shared like forebears and cheerful childhoods in different parts of the small-town South. We had both emerged into confused and partial adulthood in the twenties, combated the depression in Manhattan, separated only by streets, and we had finally met against the background of England at war, with Wert as my editor and me as his reporter on the same publication. Often we were bemused by the parallels of our pasts and the unlikely miracle of our meeting at all, and would think we understood each other better than we did. Uncovering misunderstanding, we would stand aghast in sudden loneliness the sharper because we had thought that with this marriage we had achieved unloneliness.

What else can I call it? It is a positive state of being, resulting from a negative one: the absence of loneliness.

Perhaps what we accomplished in twelve years, in spite of all our lapses—which were always succeeded by progressions—was simply the "good marriage" that almost every couple strives for; and what made it an accomplishment was, simply again, its rarity.

One brilliant spring morning at Sneden's Landing, I tried to express my delight in us after more than ten years together by making water-ground corn-meal pancakes for Wert's breakfast and by putting beside the plate as valentine a poem of Blake's, tampering only with two pronouns.

> *Love and harmony combine,*
> *And around our souls entwine*

63

While thy branches mix with mine,
And our roots together join.

Joys upon our branches sit
Chirping loud and singing sweet;
Like gentle streams beneath our feet
Innocence and virtue meet.

I the golden fruit do bear,
Thou art clad in flowers fair;
Thy sweet boughs perfume the air,
And the turtle buildeth there.

But he was cannier than I about the maintenance of what we so valued, beyond love expressed by poetry. Several days later that spring of 1953 he told me that I was trying too hard to meet the whole challenge—of life in the United States, motherhood, writing . . . and him. Fortunately, he could take me back to Europe in a month, where I couldn't cook or wash socks or worry about the community or the schools or anything *but* him, our children, and writing. "I haven't had a whole wife for several months, and to hell with it," he said. I had balanced things well for a long time, but now I was allowing the parts to add up to more than a whole, the pressures to press, the worthwhile causes to take more and more time. I realized that I was weary and diffuse and neglecting all by cutting down none of what I felt to be obligations. So, also, when we had been too long alone in Ciboure and had begun to acquire, even though together, some of the insidious laziness of hermits, he would rise one day in flight and we would go off to a capital.

Being together can be like a party where you forget for a while that you are or ever were lonely. Total revelation of yourself to another is, I suppose, possible, but I would not like to so reveal myself. It seems to me something you would have to be lonely for a while afterwards to get over. I value the deep core of my own privacy and respect that of others. "Oneness" of two people is a poet's notion. What I use the made-word "unloneliness" to try to describe is ineffable—two individuals in profound comfort together—and is, to me, the finest relationship of all.

Now, in the face of the two loneliest acts of all, dying and being left living, we tried to hold this feeling, to stay in this state.

"Dying is the last thing I'll have a chance to do well," Wert said. "I hope to hell I can."

I have a childlike, as Wert had an adult and analytical, acceptance of reality. Resignation is no part of such acceptance. I had checked and rechecked the medical questions involved in Wert's fate, and I found disagreement with Jim's psychological attitudes, but no responsible area of doubt as to his medical conclusion. So by the time Wert had returned to himself from the semi-submersion of surgery, death had moved into the middle-foreground of our lives, like a mountain, as a fact. From then on we never denied or even forgot its presence, never had to return to its existence with a sense of shock. It was no longer merely an inevitability, over the horizon, or just the possibility it had been as soon as we knew he had cancer. We used blunt, simple words when we talked about it.

Wert never became obsessed with death, any more than he ever had been. It was the end of himself as he knew himself, and it became the most important thing in his life, in ours, because it was to be soon. Everything happened in this perspective. Nothing essential had changed except the perspective. Wert did not change. Since he did not change and there was no more time to grow, he consolidated, made larger, purer, all he already was as an adult in the time he had left.

This is how he was. There is neither judgment nor conclusion in what I am writing now. Any profound experience brings you new kin. Many people have talked to me since about the dying of others. People die in as many ways as they live. Montaigne said also, in an essay called "Men by Various Ways Arrive at the Same End": "Truly man is a marvelously vain, diverse, and fluctuating subject. It is hard to found a certain and uniform judgment on him." Many die of sicknesses that directly affect the brain and the will. A doing man, in contrast to a contemplative man, may, like one I know, deliberately prefer to live his last days as if he were going to live forever. Such a man has as much right to refuse to know his fate as my man had to know his.

It is an immense subject, touching everyone. I approach writing about even the death of one man with terrified humility. Can I even convey the laughter we laughed and some of our absurd fumblings? Very few men and no women I have read think well in the abstract. There is only one piece of broad wisdom I feel justified in trying to communicate, if I can, later on. Otherwise I can only tell this story as it happened to us.

The hospital staff reacted to Wert's behavior, which changed in no particular from his normal behavior, with awe and awkwardness. They knew the result of the operation, which was on his record, and I told the friends I had made among them that he knew it, too. I hoped they would react with easy frankness toward him. Instead the opaqueness of the relationship between patient and medical attendants seemed to increase. Maybe the bell tolled too insistently on that floor. Maybe the "croakers" and "stiffs" of medical neophytes are as much fearful euphemisms as "pass on" and "gone to his reward on high."

One very pretty young nurse who believed firmly in the theory of telling patients "the worst," and with whom Wert had flirted from the beginning, with his charming Southern outrageousness, said to me, "But he's so *natural*." And Jim, shaking his head in wonder, said, "Wert hasn't changed at all. He's just exactly the same."

I began to suspect that of all attitudes the rarest is simple acceptance. It is easier perhaps to be noble than natural in the face of death.

"If *you* had been skittish—if you had lied to me by one word, by one intonation, that morning, I'd be a sniveling paranoiac by now, suspicious of everything and everybody," Wert said. It was on Friday, I think, when he marked in his *carnet,* "Better."

"You mean on Tuesday?" I asked, trying to remember what phrase I had used then to put to him the truth without a lot of words or emphasis, not even sure how conscious he was.

"No. You said 'It's not too bad' then, which was fairly ambiguous. It was enough for right then. I knew what you meant. At the time. I think I knew then anyway. It was too soon when I saw the clock, and I was conscious that stinking as I felt and much as I hurt not enough had been done to me inside. You're so far down at that point, you're pretty clear about yourself. It's later on you get confused. I was full of tubes and needles in the arm and things were being said that I couldn't hear—that whispering outside the door—and you came in and stood by the bed . . ." That was on Wednesday morning. ". . . and you said to me, 'You're going to die, but you're going to have a piece of good time first.' The truth is the whole truth as you know it and nothing else sounds the same. You were telling it and I knew it and so I felt fine. It would be no damn good for me if you hadn't. I'm a suspicious son of a bitch by nature and afraid of fooling myself or being fooled."

We decided at the time, however, to fool other people. Later we were rather sorry. It was unfair, especially to a few of them, and not Wert's way. I wish I could have been more honest with more of the people who loved Wert. It would have honored them and given them a chance to know they were saying goodbye.

Wert's strength was the kind that could only be undermined or rotted away. Mine was a kind of toughness, resilient rather than resistant, and it sprang back in response to his. Alone, or with other people, it bent under the strain. Acceptance does not obviate strain, only simplifies it. I could neither give nor accept comfort. And I was terrified of tears.

There were warning signs that I could fail Wert and then he would have to die alone. To sleep I took pills for the first time in my life. I woke up at three in the mornings, sobbing, and had to wring myself dry and take another pill. The one evening I cried in front of Suzie, who loved Wert, she immediately burst into such a flood of loving tears I realized what a mean restraint it had imposed that I had not let her weep sooner by refusing to weep myself, and that I must not get started. Later, when I had to tell three people the truth, I came out all over with hives, as I had done during the first days when I was asking for medical information on the basis of the facts.

So, for the rest, I told the whopping social lie: giving out that the operation as planned had been successfully performed. And most people believed me and those who did not most kindly did not let on. It was very restful, actually, to act out now and then the part I should have liked to be living. I'm a poor liar as a rule. Wert laughed at me for being so convincing.

"Protect yourself, honey," said Wert. "This one's on you. I need you and I'm a selfish bastard."

It's odd the tiny hazards that will nearly trip you in a planned lie. I went to one party because it was the only time I could see Teddy White before he sailed for France. Teddy was a member of that special union of us who had worked for Wert as our editor at *Time* and who had a workmen's kinship in appreciation of him. The Herseys were there, and held their heads high and stiff with me, ignoring death at the feast. The Whites were laughing over some exceedingly bawdy limericks I had written for Wert, rhyming with places we had passed through on our way across France from the Bay of Biscay to the Mediterranean, where the

Whites were living while Teddy finished his book, *Fire in the Ashes*. I said lightly, "Wert says he's going to publish a collection called *Limericks by My Wife* posthumously . . ." and stopped, stricken. It was I who would live to publish anything I might of his posthumously, to finish an article he had begun and wanted me to finish. A look from Frances Ann prompted me. I went on, ". . . and get a nice reputation as a dirty old man." Nobody else noticed the pause. Wert, for the most part, blandly refused to discuss his illness, protecting our lie with omission rather than commission, but he, too, was nearly tripped up by an unexpected word. "Tell Johnny Scott when I die he nearly caught me out with that word 'sedation,'" Wert said, later. Scott, another close member of the union, had friends in the hospital who had told him the truth and also that we both knew it. He was only trying, with love, to find out if Wert was adequately supplied with drugs, not to pry out admission with questions.

The central problem of living in Europe is to get things done. The central problem of living in the U. S. is to stop getting things done. I would come into the hospital each time from outside a little breathless, competitive, full of accomplishments: the telephone calls completed; shopping done for Christmas in Ciboure, bargains gained, too (there are no such things as bargains in France, only certain items which are sold cheaply—what they call sales are bad jokes); the bus caught just in time, or barely missed; a few friends seen; quick, so-personal exchanges with all manner of strangers; a check cashed, so easily; a prospective tenant found for our Sneden's Landing house, which was becoming unrented at this unfortunate moment; a carton of Wert's old favorite black Puerto Rican cigarettes found in a 42nd Street specialty shop as a change from his French ones. The pace of big, old, dirty, shiny, crumby, polyglot, rich, noisy, rude, friendly New York made trotting more effortless than strolling. It would take a minute to slow down and to be wholly with Wert, in the hospital room where he had established his own rhythm. Sometimes, for a minute, I would resent the change of rhythm. For one thing, I did not want to think over and separate what I had been busy at doing into those things which needed to be done and those things which had merely been done. For another, when a child has a pain, a wise old woman will jogtrot him gently to soothe him. Slow rocking is for natural sleepiness, not pain.

It was during those long, slowed-down hours in the hospital, while he was getting well enough to leave, that we learned to communicate again, with ease, thoughts that had now, of necessity, different stopping places and one poignant new restriction. No longer could we think and say to each other, Wert and I, "When we are old . . ." or even, "Next year, darling . . ." or, "It might be fun one day to go to India."

I am reminded of one of those high moments in the New York theatre. In S. N. Behrman's adaptation of Giraudoux *Amphitryon 38,* Jupiter, the immortal god, takes on the disguise of Amphitryon's mortal flesh in order to make love to Amphitryon's mortal and faithful wife. "And then suddenly," Jupiter says afterwards to his fellow god, Mercury, "she will use little expressions—and that widens the abyss between us—" "What expressions?" asks Mercury. Alfred Lunt, acting Jupiter, read the lines so tenderly that they still echo in my memory: "She will say—'When I was a child'—or 'When I'm old'—or 'Never in all my life'—This stabs me, Mercury." Then Jupiter says of gods: "But we miss something, Mercury—the poignance of the transient—the intimation of mortality—that sweet sadness of grasping at something you cannot hold—" I realize now that mortals miss it, too, when they do not seriously think about death.

We decided the near future in a brief exchange, after Jim said that Wert could leave the hospital by Thursday the

14th of October and would more than likely be fit for a boat trip by the second week in November. "A magnificent constitution—" said Jim ruefully.

"Where would you prefer me to die?" asked Wert.

"Anywhere you like," I said.

"But your first choice is Ciboure," said Wert.

"Yes," I said, "because of the children. Besides, Basques take things so flatly."

"The timing is wrong," said Wert. "I'd like a summer. This should be spring."

"Don't forget what winter in Ciboure is like, deciding," I said. "It's not comfortable."

"No. But it suits me best, anyway. I'd like the longest time possible on the sea, and then home. Then I'll know how much work I have time to do."

"A lot, maybe," I said.

"Take it easy, La-el," said Wert. "You were born cheerful."

So I called Jerry Beard, a conjurer of a travel agent who was also a friend. Could he conjure up for us, this time, a sweet, cheap little freight boat meandering toward the Mediterranean?

"There are no medical services on freight boats," warned Jerry.

"I know," I said. "Couldn't matter less."

One blessing Wert counted on impatiently was that he could dispense with all medical attention soon and for keeps. Since he had only to die, he preferred his own authority on how to do so.

With the connivance of an orderly called Joe and named Iglesias de Viñas, Wert had eschewed the indignity of bedpans in favor of painful trips out of bed. Private nursing he had dispensed with after the first sixteen hours. When his first private nurse, an elderly fuss-budget, had asked him what she could do for him in the night, he had growled, "You can sharpen up that needle you're carrying, stick it in me fast, and get out, *if* you please." The second had wanted to bathe him before breakfast, because "What would the next nurse think of me if my patient is not all cleaned up?" Wert said she could damn well think what she pleased, but the patient would damn well not be cleaned up before ten A.M. We had reduced the attention given him to a minimum, and I performed most of it. Otherwise, he tolerated the pretty or businesslike among the nurses, those with quick, competent hands—and was very fond of Joe, not because Joe was a good orderly, strong and gentle, but because he had been a *flamenco* dancer and would tap rhythms for Wert with his hands and his feet while he served him.

"I'll learn to give shots," I offered, stiffening my lip.

"Nuts. You'd push things at me and wobble," said Wert. "I'll give myself my own when I get out of here."

We would load up with pain-killers, find out how a man could dispose of himself most neatly if it became advisable, and depart on our own. So he saw it. Nothing is ever quite as it is envisioned. Nothing.

Jerry reported no freight-boat space for two years, but suggested the Export Lines, sailing by the southern route, which would land us in Cannes, France, on the Mediterranean. Wert loved the country trains that proceeded by whistle-stops along the Pyrenees to reach the other coast much better than the express trains down to our coast from the northern Atlantic ports, by way of Paris.

We could get an inside tourist cabin on the Export's *S.S. Constitution* sailing November 5th and Wert insisted that we hold this space. He did not want to wait for a better cabin on her sister ship two weeks later, although Jim was doubtful of so early a sailing as the 5th and I inclined to stay a little longer in New York, now we were there. The Gleaveses had sailed on for England, although their hearts were not light and they had wanted to cancel the trip. They had left us their spacious, comfortable house and two rooms in it were ours for as long as we would stay after they returned, for as long as they could persuade us to stay, they had said. They would be back on November 4th.

"A few hours is enough unless you really settle down with people," said Wert, "and what I'd like most now is to be on water."

I knew how he was at sea, suited by the slow-moving comfort, the sense of being suspended cozily within far horizons, the worldlessness and timelessness of shipboard. Besides, his hay fever left him on the water, and he always had an inordinate sense of well-being. The discovery of dramamine had saved me from the tendency to seasickness which marred our companionship at sea. A cabin alone, however cramped, was a home.

Wherever we spent what days we had, the cost would be roughly the same, including the small additional charge for the longer southern passage. It looked as though Wert would leave the world debtless and broke, a fair way to be. No one owed us anything, either, not even a but-for-the-grace-of-God generosity. We had been not so much improvident as high-handed. The consequences of living for the last seven years exactly as we had chosen to live were a very narrow margin of capital, a big margin of personal work done, and fine memories. Wert could easily have parlayed a few more corporate working years, at his last handsome executive salary, into a higher basic standard of living for us and a reserve bank balance, but we had taken the time instead of the money. The gamble was over, both ways, and we could not have bought time now with money. We probably had enough to get through, and sufficient insurance still in force to start me out again. We felt fortunate. And so the gifts people gave us were luxuries.

One I demanded, free to demand anything of Benjamin Sonnenberg because he did exactly as he pleased, for his pleasure or profit, and could not be imposed upon. He handled public relations for the Export Lines, so I called him now.

"Tell your guy he's the only man in the world I love well enough to visit in a hospital," said Ben. "I'm ordering a fleet of cars at once and I'll arrive in state this afternoon."

"He doesn't love you well enough," I said. "He wouldn't receive the angel Gabriel in a hospital. See that we have a private bathroom on that ship of yours, and I'll love you forever."

Ben snorted, I think. We had known each other as many years as he and Wert had known each other, which was more than twenty-five. Wert had never asked him a favor, although part of Ben's business was the multitudinous granting of favors in return for others. Years ago, during the depression, I had asked Ben to help me find a job, which he had. Ben preferred to confer cases of liquor, and liked to impose his own generosities. He suggested books, flowers, and champagne.

I told him Wert had read everything, had hay fever and wasn't drinking yet, and I wanted that can for him. Ben laughed and called me a "Coca-Cola girl." Wert, he said, was a gentleman, adding that this was a rare thing to be.

Having no notion whether he would do anything about our accommodations, I invited Ben for tea when Wert was out of the hospital, which he countered with an invitation to dinner at his house.

The few other people I called—only a few, for there was so little time, and I confined the calls to dwellers in Manhattan—also wanted to know what they could do or send. I could truthfully say we wanted nothing.

I waited to call Max Ascoli, editor of the *Reporter*. Whatever I did not tell him, I must convey to Max the sad fact that there would be no more contributions from Wert to his magazine, no further series on Spain, no taking on of a vast writing puzzle such as the China Lobby issue. Max called me instead, and when his voice, with its Italian accent and its spaced *mmmms,* professorial and affectionate, came over the wire saying urgently, "Tell me, Lael, how is dear Charlie?" I could not lie to his intuitiveness. I said that I would come to his house to see him and his wife, Marion, for we wives were the closest of friends. I told them, then, and Marion said, "Oh, the end of something good is so hard!"

There was only one problem in relation to the future that distressed Wert past acceptance, that made him feel fearful and guilty: as if he had, in this one way, by coming to death now, failed his inheritors.

"Listen," I had said once to Wert when we were discussing our precarious finances, "if you put Chris in a cave, he'd find a way to get educated. His curiosity is as much part of him as the brains to satisfy it. As to whether Miss Timberlake should be educated at all, that's a moot point."

It was a light-hearted attitude we could share when we were merely broke and knew that Wert could go into the magazine market, where he commanded general respect, and get assignments when we needed eating money, or later tuition for schools and colleges. Watching them grow, we had observed how much better off both children were when they were challenged and put to it by the schools they were in. They both responded with alacrity, enthusiasm, effort and top marks to the stern standards and the reverence for academic excellence found in France.

It does not matter what tongue a village speaks to childhood, if it is a healthy, free-spoken tongue, and speaks warmly. A second language, a breadth of view, naturally acquired as only children can acquire them, are fine things to have. However, we felt strongly that our young should be educated in their own country, in the United States, when the time came to learn also exactly who and what they were, in adolescence. We wanted, perhaps greedily, to help them keep and increase the sound classical basis European schools offered, especially as we had been embattled all our lives against our own lack of such a basis. We wanted them best trained, too, in their own country, for whatever they might choose to do. In spite of efforts to find and encourage them, we knew that many first-class brains were lost to adequate training through the sprawling carelessness of the American educational system, and because of too little money available at the key moments of decision.

"We'll manage," I assured Wert now. But I did not want him to need such reassurance. It was a negative need, nagging, irksome, not good.

It was as if the negative need called forth the positive response. An unexpected call from a peripatetic friend came in because somewhere he had heard a rumor. . . . "*Are* you in trouble?" he asked. "Please remember that for people like me giving help is no hardship. So *don't be silly.*" Without telling Wert ahead of time, I saw him and told him the one thing that was fretting a man he cherished who was the father of children. "I may not need help," I said. "But Wert needs peace of mind," he replied, "and whether you'll need it or not is beside the point. To me it's not charity, but a privilege. It's settled. So don't tell anyone else because these things are private affairs, but please go tell Wert at once. Right this minute."

When I finished telling him how this friend had, with joy and grace, insisted on his right to help Wert's children later if I could not manage alone, Wert said, "How good people can be! What a wonderful thing." He felt an elation that was more than his own relief. It was identification with goodness and gracious behavior, more than just through personal friendship, through common humanity. There were also, for the second time I had ever seen them, tears on his face.

Now we were once more embarked on a course of action for as far ahead as we could see. Minor decisions had been made, Wert's major worry about our future without him had been eliminated, his last night as an institutionalized body instead of a free man was passed and we set out together from the hospital.

I had seen by then several departures from the hospital floor and ours was very like the others.

The patient's clothes never quite fit. They are from "before," and he resembles a man self-consciously returning to civilian clothes after a long time in uniform. He moves precariously, but ignores, with a pretense at irritation, the solicitous hovering of the next-of-kin, who is fatuous and fusses. The farewells are warm, but absent-minded, the enforced and unreal intimacy is over, and the participants in this leave-taking will more than likely never see each other again. For some reason, a bed is always moved by with a very ill patient upon it just as the convalescent is moving on shaky legs toward his release. The elevator operator knows, by now, the next-of-kin and has read on her face rather than in her answers the progress of the patient's illness. The patient is a stranger to him and he does not respond to an introduction, although he pretends to. The patient pushes at the revolving door downstairs, but it is the next-of-kin who forces it to go around and deposit them on the street. The patient blinks, startled, fills his lungs with the polluted but heady air of freedom, calls "Taxi," and is immediately a contender, no quarter offered, for the rewards normal life offers. Upon giving the driver a street address, he is in charge of his own fate again, and no longer a patient.

When we reached our gift house, Wert quickly made himself at home on the second floor, where he had bedroom and bath and where the spacious living room looked out over a minuscule, autumnal Manhattan garden. I went down to the kitchen and made tea. We were at home for three weeks more in New York, until the ship sailed to take us back home to Ciboure.

Wert made a note for *The Time of Enchantment:* "A man finds a home and leaves it, because safety softens him, and in-

77

tends to return. When his home is in conflict, there may be no return, and so the safety and the softness compound each other, and he may lose the capacity to free himself." Freedom from conflict, freedom to leave, freedom to return . . .

Jim called to see us that afternoon, to check on Wert, to give prescriptions and instructions. He said, "I have never seen a man hold himself straighter, with heavy stitches still in such an incision."

I telephoned Max afterwards, to tell him how Wert was, as he had asked me to do.

"How is Charlie taking it?" asked Max. "I mean . . . knowing . . ."

Wert was standing in the doorway and I looked at him.

"Arrogantly," I said.

7

If a man lived vitally, Samuel Butler reckoned for him a further life after death of threescore more years and ten in the minds of some who had known him, and perhaps a little longer if he had written well enough. Wert was not concerned with immortality, spiritual or literary, but only with this kind of mortality: he believed that the good he was and had done would outlive him and the evil die quickly, and the essence of good and evil and the nature of truth were what he had lived the last years of his life trying to know.

Perhaps the time has come to look at Charles Wertenbaker from the viewpoint of other people, as he was seen by the world in which he left his memory.

When we discussed the extended mortality which is memory in the minds of others, Wert said I exaggerated his effect on others. If he had seen the letters which confirmed me in this, he would have been pleased, but would have pointed out that there was a high percentage of professional literacy among those we knew best and that furthermore all such letters, however sincere, are flowers, selected, weeded, and stripped of thorns.

He was not in the least a humble man, but he had an acute and deflating sense of proportion. We had both taken at this time to reading obits and noting the ages and causes of death among strangers. When we confessed this to each other, Wert remarked that such notices were disproportionately long and glowing for members of the writing fraternity. It is a temptation to quote here from articles as well as obits and letters, to include Brendan Gill's review of *The Death of Kings* from the *New Yorker,* and Max Ascoli's column on Wert's dying from the *Reporter.* I am nibbling at this temptation when I mention them. There was an article in Basque, too, a language in which a man other than another Basque has rarely been mentioned except in anger, and a *jota* written in Zaragoza to "El Periodista Magnífico Carlos Cristian," with a scribbled apology that the name Wertenbaker did not lend itself to poetry or music. Wert would not only have told me to put them all back in the folder I keep for his children's pride in him, which is immense, but would have warned me to be careful not to add to his stature by any cubit of my loving selectivity. He would have pointed out that this best and most understanding review had critical counterparts; Max was also a friend; the tribute in Basque sounded as if it was written to him because of his highly honored position in the Basque community, but the prime inspiration for it was a Basque journalist's son who went swimming with us and who called Wert "Pape," as did most of Chris's friends. The song resulted not only from admiration for Wert's contribution to international understanding of Spain but also from a marvelously drunken evening with a Spanish editor as host.

It does not seem to me, after reflection, that I can fairly represent any viewpoint other than my own. I could never balance sources and do a "profile" of Charles Christian Wertenbaker, anyway. When Wert did one such of Edward R. Murrow, three paragraphs into which he had packed his own warm opinion of his friend Ed were excised as "too personal." I still think the profile immeasurably less accurate for that editing. Would this, on the other hand, be more just if I tried to be judicious? The opinions of other women, about which I could scarcely be fair, would have to take into account the extent and character of their relations with him,

Suppose I quoted an argument between a colleague who liked him and a colleague who did not, at *Time,* the one maintaining that he was the ideal editor who hired adults in a free enterprise and respected his employees and himself in their mutual search for truth, the other insisting that he was lazy, and soft-minded, and spoiled his workmen? Wert worked for Time, Inc., a total of sixteen years, was thrice hired and thrice fired, and held positions varying from animals editor to foreign editor of *Time.* Henry Luce's letter to me later bridged these years and the years after with the grace of his sense of loss, respect, and affection for a man who had often been his vital antagonist. Wert would have felt the same if Luce had died, but such a residue at the end of it does not explain the complex of their working and personal relationship. In this form, personal and far short of biography, I think I must properly keep to the impacts made by the succeeding moments in this period.

Those last visits of friends to the house on 61st Street are misty. There was the triple opaqueness for me of my lying, "behaving well" because there wasn't any other way to behave that I could figure, and my distracted inattention. I remember only the faces of those days sharply, from Rose Burgener's loving Italian imp's countenance, through the beautiful Gleaveses returning with their hearts in their faces. Wert did not consider that there was sufficient time for them to settle with and so to talk in terms of death. Indeed, two who had guessed that he was dying were "redeceived." I think they all, as Orson Welles expressed it in a letter, "rejoiced in that gaiety, which—since it was clearly a matter of some highly serious private decision, the very opposite of caprice—we found so overwhelmingly flattering." I remember when Frances Ann Hersey walked in, rigid with emotion, how Wert tackled her immediately on what she, four times delivered of child, did about the indecent itching of shaven pubic hair and how she responded with bawdy wit. Wert created, in that living room, an atmosphere, as he usually managed to do, so that all conversation was over a low wooden fence in the backyard of eternity.

If I felt, as I did, that each visit was a gift, a bequest, to the visitor, those I agonized over not inviting because time was tighter than affection will understand, and those who came will forgive my manner almost of "presenting" them. "You do exaggerate my importance," Wert said, and laughed at me, and continued to behave as if these partings were no different from others in a profession where it was the convention merely to wave a hand as you left for China. He was serene and casual and never then or later felt the need to say farewell to anyone or anything nor wished to impose a "last" impression.

Occasionally he gave me a message to send afterwards. When Lillian Hellman left, he said: "Tell Lil I bequeath you her friendship. A very valuable loyal thing. I'm glad I can." He knew as I did that friendship cannot be bequeathed without consent. As a widow, I hoped I would not want compassionate friendship, and Wert did not think I would. Some relationships would change wholly and all of them some. "Tell her, too, how damn sorry I was not to tell her, of all people, the truth. Write her before she writes you." After his editor from Random House, Robert Linscott, and later his agent, Ivan von Auw, had been there, he said: "Tell 'em not to begrudge me the marvelous pleasure of talking like that about a book I won't be able to write." In a commercial era and country, the granite New England integrity of the man who was his chosen editor, and the nervous, sensitive, partisan courage of his agent had been an integral part of his years of living and writing as he pleased. After John Scott: "You can count on him, Lael." After Willie Walton: "Save your early Waltons. I think he'll paint better and better."

Three people, as if by instinct, brought their sons to meet him: Mary Bancroft's twenty-five-year-old, Ben Sonnenberg's seventeen-year-old, and the Michael Bessies' frisky three.

"Another generation," wrote Connie Bessie later, "enriched by a teaparty."

Except at night with Wert alone, my attention was nervously divided and much of it was elsewhere. Cooking for Wert was simple, since he felt like eating simply, and housekeeping, in the absence of the Gleaveses' helper during their absence, was made simple by the prodigal gift of Nancy White's cleaning woman twice a week. But research on "how to die without making a mess of it if you want to," which I was doing for Wert, was not simple, and collecting drugs to take back to France was not.

Jim was worried because Wert's pain did not diminish as the stitches came out and the incision healed well. Reluctantly he admitted that the cancer was probably encouraged by its airing and in estimating the amount of drugs it would take to carry us through he admitted also, with the shyest reluctance, that the amount did not vary much with the amount of time we should have. More pain, more drugs— more cancer, less time. I also fished out of Jim his most reluctant opinion that morphine itself was the best and safest killer and an idea of how much "not to take." Both of us were unreasonably irked by Jim's unwillingness to say too much. He would have done anything for us that was not against his own deepest conscience.

Finally my aunt and uncle helped me to get a treatise on morphine written for doctors only, and Wert and I felt fortified by its length and technical detail. It sounded definitive. We were preparing determinedly, not for suicide, but against prolonged dying until man was body and not man.

Jim had offered, and tried, to get the whole supply of dolophine, a substitute Wert was using as long as possible, and morphine, for us. His druggist legitimately turned him down. Only a limited supply at a time per patient was permitted by law. Legal morphine is cheap and plentiful. The laws were designed to prevent a hideous traffic. We never then or later made any effort to acquire any drugs from tainted sources, not wishing to make any kind of contribution to such traffic. The laws were proper, but they were not written to prevent extensive use of morphine in such a case. To circumvent the pure legality of this situation, Jim provided me with a fistful of prescriptions with which I must walk the streets from drugstore to drugstore having them filled one at a time. Beginning to trudge from the very notion of how much trudging it would take, I saw on a corner one of those old-fashioned pharmacist's windows. Over the window and door was a gold-lettered sign in gothic script reading: *Thomas E. Bradford, Druggist. Established 1876.* I went in and asked for Mr. Bradford.

Medium-sized and sandy-complected, Mr. Bradford was a man of meticulous manners and visible rectitude. I showed him my prescriptions and told him my problem.

"My dear, if you will go back to Dr. Danielson and get a single prescription I shall have the full supply ready for you tomorrow afternoon. I wish to have a single prescription because I should not care for anyone to think I was attempting any deception."

"What about the narcotics inspectors?" I asked him.

Mr. Bradford, a man whom you could not visualize selling an ice-cream soda or peddling so much as a grain of aspirin for any but proper purposes, said, "*I* will deal with the inspectors. God bless you."

I reflected gratefully upon the freedom and courage of incorruptible men and Wert went by later to shake hands with him.

There was also the problem of taking the drugs into France, but this did not worry either of us. Our theory about smuggling was that, for the demi-innocent and nonprofessional anyway, the customs men would find what they were looking for and ignore what they were not. Out of politeness, you hid things a bit, but you didn't feel as if you were outsmarting anyone as a rule. Jim almost upset this by his loving concern. Without asking us, he called the Federal Narcotics Bureau and asked as our surgeon for permission for us to carry drugs. The answer was an emphatic no. "We might," said an officer in the department, "in view of such medical circumstances, get permission from the U.S. government in about three months, Doctor, but we would never get it from the French. It is a serious offense to take drugs out of, or into, a country."

So I telephoned the officer. "I just want to know," I said carefully, "in view of your reply, whether I can carry enough to take care of my husband on the trip. For the rest, I shall have to get it—of course—in France." I knew damn well how hard it was to get enough in France. I remembered a wealthy retired dentist living in St. Jean-de-Luz who had died of cancer and how I avoided the block in which he lived during the weeks before he died because at intervals his screaming could be heard from behind the closed windows of his house.

"You may *not*," said the officer gruffly. "It is *strictly against the law*. You can go to prison. You may not carry any with you *at all*."

"Then I shall have to get what we must have from the doctor on the ship," I said.

"Yes," said the officer. "And—may I say I'm sorry, Mrs. Wertenbaker, about your husband? And wish you both—luck."

That's all I wanted to know, bless him. Whatever he could not do or say, he could refrain from listing our name to be watched at the ports of exit, and he had.

So we were protected against the enemy, the octopus, with small, white, powerful pills (which, to be polite, we put in vitamin-pill bottles) and against the friendly enemy, the narcotics law, in case the pills were inadvertently discovered and recognized, with a letter from Jim, which he did not want me to show Wert.

To Whom It May Concern:
Mr. Charles Wertenbaker was operated upon by me at

the ———————— Hospital on October 5th, 1954. He has carcinoma of the cecum which has metastasized to numerous areas in the peritoneum, as well as to the liver. The patient has need for increasing amounts of morphine and its derivatives. A plentiful supply has been made available. Both his hospital records and my own are readily available for inspection with permission of the patient or his wife.

There were some strenuous extraneous incidents, such as the baked potato that exploded all over the kitchen. There was a trip out to Sneden's Landing, where I got from the attic some thick long woolen underwear Wert had worn during the war on the cold front of the Bulge, and a strong, curve-handled cane from his cane-carrying days. There was an unexpected audition downtown of some songs for which I had done the lyrics. Wert insisted that I tend to this, unimportant as it seemed to me then, because he wanted to know that *A Man Is Born,* which had been written to him, would be sung one day by somebody other than me. There was the evening we ventured out, to hear the last two acts of Wert's favorite opera, *Der Rosenkavalier,* from which Wert returned, as he always had, singing the Baron Ochs role in his inaccurate belly-bass and burlesquing the burlesque waltz of the Baron's, his arm held as if in a sling.

The deeply moving weekend with his older son, Bill, in whom man was emerging from boy, came near the end.

Since we had returned to France in 1953, Wert had not pressed the legal claim which entitled him to a major share in Bill's summers. Wert felt that Bill had come of an age to be offered his choice, and that it was natural, at fifteen and sixteen, for him to choose the familiar vacation pleasures of Gloucester, Massachusetts, with his mother, his grandmother and his sailboat. The boy Bill who had been with us in France earlier had not liked France, and now the man was thinking, as Wert had expected he would come to think, that he would like it very much and that he had been missing his father more than he knew. He was looking forward to next summer with his Pop and with us. "The timing's all wrong," Wert said to me when Bill had gone back to school. They had been so pleased with each other and so easy together. "It would have been simpler for him if I'd died either sooner or later. Don't let him fret about missing anything he might have had—it was natural it happened that way. And do what you can. You two like each other. I'd like Chris and Timberlake and Bill to have each other. I'm sorry as hell to pull out on him right now."

Wert's younger sister, Imogen, came up from Charlottesville for a day. Later she told me she knew intuitively but would not say she knew because acknowledgment was up to us. "I was so glad my brother had found everything he wanted in life, which was a lot, before he died," she said. When I asked her what she wanted of his, she said, "To know his children."

On the last day, the Gleaveses came back from England, and Chrissie and Jack Ratcliff came in from Sneden's Landing with their thirteen-year-old daughter, Alex. The Ratcliffs' was the house to which our house had once been the stable. Their older daughter, Lydia, had lived with us two summers when the Ratcliffs went away and closed up next door, and was a member of our family. Alex had been in love with Wert since she was nine years old. At one time she kept in her dresser drawer a doll representing me into which she stuck voodoo pins in the hope that I would die and she could have him undivided. Later we made friends. The Ascolis came, for the last time, my aunt and uncle, Lil Hellman again, and, that night, the Herseys.

I remember John Hersey, tall, reticent, not a man to communicate his emotions directly, stopping short in his leave-taking and saying tightly, "You make me want to write!"

Then downstairs at the door they each held me hard and went out together, almost running.

Wert said to me, "Tell John one day that I leave with him all my faiths—no, all my *certainties*—of good."

John wrote a letter which reached Ciboure on January 2nd expressing the meaning of the moment and the years, and I am very glad Wert had it when it meant the most to him.

Dear Wert:

It is Christmas day, and I want to write you. I have not been a good letter-writer, ever; there's not much use saying I'm sorry.

The Christmas tree part of Christmas day went through here rather rapidly. The children had everything unwrapped and were ready for whatever comes after Christmas (and that's a problem in itself) at 8:35 A.M. You are a man to appreciate that statistic.

Our children devised a skit for a four-family Christmas Eve party last night: The History of Man, beginning with the earliest stage of evolution—the Glob; the fish, the ape, cave man, and so on, up to man's greatest triumph, television; then the same stages in reverse, all watching T.V., ending with a fascinated Glob. Very funny. Johnny, Jr. printed this stationery. For money he did. Letters have come from two more ex-Time Incers who say free-lancing doesn't pay. . . . It is all the same. I am working very hard on two books at once. It is fair and colder.

My dear, calm friend!

Why did we four have such good times together? It couldn't have been just that you and Frances Ann had such sugar-mouths (ha!) and that Lael and I were the spawnings of preachers and missionaries. How Frances Ann and I admired your and Lael's guts—or maybe it was just being yourselves and whole-hearted—when you pulled up stakes six or seven years ago or whenever it was and went to live there in Ciboure.

I've been wanting to find something better to say than

'You make me want to write,' but I can't. When that came out impulsively, I was afraid it sounded as if I'd merely heard a little clatter of that old winged chariot. Just a slight shudder and a feeling of hurry. No, that wasn't what I meant! I meant much more. I meant the same thing that happens when I read certain very few things: I want to write. It is the finest feeling, because then I can a little, when I see the best. You are noble. Do you expect me to sit here and say nothing? You manage to make a kind of dance of it. I admire you and envy you. I want to write and I will write something good for you, my old editor, my good friend.

At the proper time, give Natty Bumpo our love, and Mozart, and Dick, and Dr. Frazier and old Bladderfill, and other great ones. We love you truly and you live in us truly and forever.

John

On Friday, the 5th of November, we left New York and went up the gangplank onto the *S.S. Constitution*. Parting from us at the doorway of her hospitable house, Suzie had said, "A ship leaving shore undoes me—without any other complications. I love you." Charlie Gleaves went with us and helped us board, arguing in the manner of a students' bull session, although with many more years' worth of wisdom, with Wert, who had been his classmate at the University of Virginia, about Lord Melbourne. Ben Sonnenberg, a perfectionist when he chose to do a personal favor, had arranged an outside room for us, with bathroom, in cabin class. We had no clothes or taste for the social life of first class at the time, and Wert, who had already taken two of the white pills that morning, need not now cope with tourist class, full as it was of exuberant collegians and prolific Italian families. We went on deck when the whistle sounded its doom-like roar and the ship began to shudder and move. Gleaves on the dock was waving and waving from his great height, behind the crowd. The ship started in stately leisure down the great river, farther up the other shore of which was our own roof. Wert leaned on his cane and watched the buildings and then the Statue until they diminished behind us.

"What *are* you humming?" he asked me. My tunes are apt to be indistinguishable.

"I used to know it once," I said. "The refrain's half-stuck in my head . . . *'Oh it ain't so mighty far to the goodbye gate, my honey, my love . . . But it's a mighty far piece to the farewell lane, my honey . . . my love . . . my heart's delight. . . . My honey, my love!'*"

Wert stretched and smelled the salt in the air with satisfaction.

"Let's take one turn around the deck, put in for chairs, and then go get ready for lunch," he said, sounding very happy.

8

When we planned trips, my enthusiasm usually lagged behind Wert's. I never wanted, was quite ready, to leave home. I knew the children had never suffered from our bursts of absence, that I should work better upon returning for having been away, that I should be glad I was wherever we went and pleased to have been there afterwards, but I was still reluctant to go. When we planned to start for home, at the end of being somewhere else, my enthusiasm outran his. When we actually set out, in any direction, for anywhere, our exhilarations matched.

We were companionably exhilarated that first afternoon and night on shipboard.

After lunch, as soon as we had traded in an armchair covered with slippery, bright-colored imitation leather for a man-sized lounge chair with deep, cloth-covered cushions, we were comfortable. After I had unpacked, spreading our minimal possessions lavishly in drawer and locker space for four, we were settled. Henry, a sympathetic Chilean who had arranged the chair exchange and was our steward, brought a bucket of ice mid-afternoon. There were huge bronze chrysanthemums, a fruit basket, candy and cookies, a leather lap board with magnetic pencil and metal clip, telegrams, books, and a case of champagne. The cabin looked festive.

"Ah, now," said Wert.

When he noticed that my activities had become the fidgetings of a housewife, a sort of domestic dromomania, he said, *"You* sit down!"

This, he expounded, dolophine and champagne combining to make him immediately a little drunk, was not borrowed time, but free time, shipboard time, which could never be prosy no matter how prosy it was—good waste time. I was looking all worn out, and small wonder, and I was to stop thinking, fretting, stewing, worrying, or doing, for eight free days. Rest, eat, drink—as much as my poor old liver, beaten up by hepatitis three years before, would allow—and make a little quiet merry.

"Tant pis for your liver," he said, with majestic superiority. "Now *I* intend to get very agreeably drunk, having just an eensy teensy bit of cancer in mine."

"Just the *'least* little bit pregnant,'" I said, quoting a whiskery joke.

"Exactly. So put another bottle of this excellent Bollinger on ice before we repair to the bar to drink old-fashioneds for my cold."

This was a family joke. It came from the night when George Waller, then Minister to Luxembourg, and a hearty Virginia drinker, had said: "Let us mix another shaker of martinis before we switch to whiskey for Mr. Wertenbaker's cold."

"If you catch cold, I'll leave you," I said irrelevantly, repeating an old threat. Wert was a monster when he had one of his rare and monstrous colds.

This foolish dialogue, which I remember so literally, gave me the impulse to rise from where I had stretched out on the berth and go over to touch him as he rose from his chair to fill my glass. We met, touched, kissed, intending it lightly, and were both caught in emotion so intense and spontaneous that the brevity of our actions only contributed to the moment's perfection. The tears ran out of the sides of my eyes into my ears and hair afterwards, not in sorrow, but as they did once in a long time with wonder at such emotion so confirmed by a simple, universal act.

Then Wert dropped his head, after a luminous look, and said quietly, "I think that's the last time, my dear love. That took everything I had. That's all I've got."

His exhaustion had finality about it. It was a long time before he could get up, dress again, and put a second bottle on the ice.

We went to the bar much later and then to dinner, where we found the menu more promising than the food, and then to the lounge for coffee, and then down again. We talked tranquilly, until midnight, for once, caught us both in the act of falling asleep as suddenly as children do, mid-sentence.

Wert kept track of the dolophine he was taking. He wanted to be very careful not to build up a resistance to this drug and to be forced over to morphine. I glanced at the page of his date-book in the morning and saw that he had needed dolophine at 2:45 A.M. and at 6:00 A.M. I had slept across the narrow cabin from him so buried in unconsciousness that I had not heard him stir. I wondered whether I should worry about this. Then I became uncertain whether I could worry even if I should. Wert was in the shower and steam was coming into the cabin through the open bathroom door. Feeling cold, I closed the door and turned up the heat control on the air conditioner.

As soon as he came in, Wert turned it down. "What's the matter with you anyway?" he asked.

"Nothing," I said. "Lethargic. Dramamine, maybe."

Wert looked impatient and I tried to hurry dressing, but only succeeded in misplacing everything I touched. Before we went out, Wert hesitated and then took another dolophine.

On deck it was cold, but the sun shone. So that Wert could be undisturbed, we had chosen a place for our deck chairs beside a barred entry to stairs that seemed to lead to the bowels of the ship and were only for use by the personnel. People, the decorous-mannered people of cabin class, walked by and by again as we lay there, wrapped in blankets, side by side. Occasional tentative smiles offered friendly exchanges or to let us alone as we wished to be. We could hear subdued shouts and the sound of pounding feet from another part of the deck where games were being played. When the bouillon was served, Wert used it to wash down another pill.

Several times I started to make a remark, but the effort seemed immense and I desisted.

Wert turned to me and said something. I said, after a pause: "What?" He made a face. Ordinarily I should have told him to speak up or hush up, and laughed at him for muttering. If he doubted the importance of what he was saying, he was inclined to speak indistinguishably, and the less important it was the more he resented repeating it. I only said, "What?" again, hearing my voice querulous, and offered an inert, desperate attention when he repeated himself.

We seemed to be trying to reach each other through a mist. The mist emanated from me. The day was like a bad dream of separation and search. All vision and sound were distorted and blurred, all effort turned back upon itself and was futile. Screams would have been soundless. I remember a rent in the mist that was a flash of terror and how the mist seemed to close around me again and all feeling was blurred into no feeling. I talked and Wert said, angrily, "You're just talking." I was silent and Wert said, "You're not here. You're somewhere I can't get at you." I made occasional gestures of affection, and Wert rejected them as what they were—empty.

In the past there had been plenty of days, even periods, when Wert and I were not in more than superficial communication with each other. There is a certain stage of a book when any novel writer has gone to live in his self-created world and is absent except in the flesh from the one he eats, sleeps and loves other people in. There were other times when speech between us was like smoke-signals from hilltops with a valley in between them. It was not reasonable to suppose that we should always operate on the same level of intimacy, and we did not suppose so.

But over this day there was a sense of doom, of eternal separation. Perhaps in living with death so frankly and even impudently, we had dared death, which was stronger than we were. If, for these final, irreplaceable days, I could only act at the part of a good and loving wife, Wert would never be audience or actor in a play. I knew that I no longer felt pain or joy or worry or love, only a kind of zombie fear, as if I had held my silly head so stiffly my foolish neck had broken and I was a chicken's body of dead reflexes.

The day was neither long nor short for me, only empty and remotely dreadful. Night came and I could go to bed, with the final meager pretense that I would sit in bed and try to talk. I drowned in sleep very early, and Wert sat up until 4:15, tempering pain and loneliness with drugs and whiskey.

He, who had approached this last part of his life eagerly, wanting to make of it for us something better than just days tacked onto his life, had he committed the final act of *hubris* and must he learn at the end that every man is wholly alone?

The next morning when I opened my eyes it was timidly. As soon as Wert was awake, I went over and touched his cheek. He looked at me a minute, blinking. The mist was gone.

Henry managed to get us a pot of black Italian coffee and breakfast was a pleasure.

"I feel like a collection of limbs that had been left around in the bottom of a rain barrel," I said, deeply grateful that those limbs were no longer insentient.

"You were just tired out," said Wert. "Relaxing like I told you to. I should have let you alone."

"No, you shouldn't have," I said. "I was in a coma."

"Dopey day," said Wert somberly.

It was all right if it had been only a single day because it was over. We clasped hands, making a compact without words against anything that could separate us: cowardice, fear, pretense, weariness, pain, even sympathy.

That Sunday was everything we had hoped for the trip. It was a serene and beautiful day. An ample autumn sun shone from a light blue sky onto a dark blue ocean. Single white cloud idling in sky, single white ship swaying on ocean. Wert took his cane and we paced the deck, my hand inside the crook of his elbow. At lunch the headwaiter offered to fix us his chafing-dish specialties and they were delicious. We took a siesta and both slept. After tea, on deck in our chairs, we felt a limitless mutual contentment containing within it the cores of each one's separate distress. Wert found that his pain stayed under the level where it disturbed him if he took half pills of dolophine more frequently instead of whole ones at longer intervals. I recognized the coma of yesterday as a coma of escape. Today I seemed to have learned to balance present against future and to allow Wert to die for me not a thousand times, but only once.

Wert exclaimed: "I've got a wonderful, corny idea. Why not? This ship goes on to Genoa and Naples and then back to Cannes. 'See Naples and die!'"

"Corny and wonderful," I said, and went off to see the purser.

It proved to be feasible. We should have to leave the ship entirely while she was in harbor at Naples, but we could leave our luggage aboard and our "valuables" in a locked box with the purser. That meant we should not have to risk our drugs through customs in Italy, nor their discovery by a maid when our cabin was changed. It would cost us nothing to go on to Naples and the cost of returning to Cannes by the same ship was small. I could telegraph or perhaps telephone home our change of plans from Gibraltar, our first stop. Wert had long wanted to go to Naples, which we had missed on our trips to Italy, proscribed as they were by the articles he did to finance them.

By the light of a huge, romantic, sea-borne moon that night, it seemed more than ever like a fine idea to "See Naples . . ."

There were signs that night which we interpreted, in our still vast medical ignorance, as gains by the enemy, the octopus, in his battle for possession of Wert's once beautiful body. His abdomen had swelled perceptibly during the day and was hot to the touch. The long scar with its stitchmarks had widened and tightened. One testicle was very swollen and his graceful, small-boned ankles were as misshapen as an obese old woman's.

"God, I'm hideous," said Wert, looking at his body with disgust.

"Are you comfortable?" I asked, adding, I think, something about no time for vanity, and that he had been more spare and splendid than most men for more years.

He was comfortable, he said, but the pain was increasing, under the drug. "If it keeps on at this rate, I don't think I've a hell of a lot more time. Would it be too grim for you if I died on shipboard or in Naples?" In his dressing gown, he was prowling the cabin, anxious and affectionate, reconsidering the extra days it would take to go on to Naples and return.

It did not seem to me to matter where. It was so secondary. I wanted to tell him exactly how I felt so that he would know and would be freed to do as he pleased.

"I would rather, a little, Ciboure. But it's unimportant. If it's all the same to you, I'll get you back there, anyway, one way or the other."

Then we had the conversation that settled everything that could be thus settled between us.

If he were buried in the Ciboure cemetery, overlooking the bay, which he loved, it would give his children a piece of earth in that part of the world, and it would belong to them always. Otherwise he favored the sea. It was such a clean and decent thing for a body to go into the sea and its return to the elements was quicker and simpler. Cremation, for some reason, displeased us both, in the abstract.

"Whatever you want, you may have," I said as refrain. "But if it's all the same to you, if you should die on board or on land, I'll take you back."

"Wouldn't it be a nightmare trip and aren't there all kinds of legalities?" asked Wert.

We both remembered Marie Anne Eheremendy, after she had ridden down in the hearse which carried her *douanier* husband's body from the state hospital in Paris to his home in Sare, near us. It was a haunting thought, that trip of hers; she had been nearly destroyed by it.

"Nevertheless," I said, "I'll get you back, unless you prefer the sea."

Wert, still prowling and pacing, as he did when he was pondering, said, "I don't want to get back to Ciboure a mess of a dying man. I'd rather leave the kids as I left them unless I can have some good time with them. I don't want them to have any feeling of horror. And I never saw the point to dramatic farewells. If you haven't been and done and said what you wanted to, it's too late."

"They won't *see* you the way grownups do," I said. "Kids don't. They take appearances for granted unless somebody confuses them."

Wert agreed to this. They might be aware, momentarily, of how thin his face was, but probably that was all. There was something else on his mind, more urgent now because he was so aware of his rapid disintegration. "If I should happen to decide to go overboard myself because that still appeals to me, you know, would you mind?"

I did not mind anything except that he must die, and I told him so. It would take a little bit longer to get it straight with the children, why and how it had been, but it could be made straight with them. "All I should like to ask is to *know* if you decide to," I told him.

"You're sure?" asked Wert. He stood as far away from me as he could get when he asked this and spoke very coolly, as if he would prefer a different answer.

"Yes," I said.

"Or if I do it any other way?"

"*Yes.*"

"You mustn't ever say you knew or touch anything, you know."

"Don't worry about me afterwards, about things like that, darling love!" I said. "I'll get a certificate of natural death if I can. Otherwise if anyone asks me anything I won't know anything and if necessary I can always have hysterics. No one will want to make trouble for me, so they won't. But I want to know."

"You're *sure* sure you want to know?" Wert asked.

"*Sure* sure," I said.

Then he came over and put his hands around my face. "I can see right through you!" he exclaimed. "Your face is all love."

The next morning I had to help him to get his shoes on his swollen feet. He could hardly bend over the swelling of his abdomen and the fever-heat of it was intense. Having settled with and for this new physical condition of things, Wert made no comment on it other than to say I made an awkward valet. He took his cane and we went up two flights in the elevator to go on deck in the brilliant morning sun. I confirmed with the purser that we should be going on to Naples. Wert suggested that I get my hair done while he had a haircut. Since we did not look at anyone much except each other, we might as well look our best. Although, he added, cheerfully insulting, I always looked like a peeled onion with my hair fresh done, but that would wear off by the next day.

"I'm sorry I have such a battered old pan," I apologized.

"Since I gave you most of your wrinkles," said Wert, "I find them rather endearing and I like your hair going gray. So if I like it, stop fussing."

"The aging romantics," I said.

"I'm always romantic on shipboard," said Wert. "Like spring."

Wert loved the form of the year. He said he had fallen in love every spring every year but one since he was fourteen. As regularly, he stopped loving life and people every February. It was the womb of the year for him, the month in which he had been born, struggling out of darkness, the month he did penance for the other eleven. The summer brought him sweat and laziness and the ability to lie for hours immobile in the sun. In autumn he was full of vigor, male, driving, and creative. Winter brought him fireside contemplation and new philosophies. And every spring (except that one), emerging from February reborn, since we had fallen first in love on the grass at Oxford in England in the spring, he had fallen in love again each year with the same woman, with me. It was different from loving.

"There's a full moon Wednesday," I said. "How about falling in love again this fall instead of waiting for spring?"

"Don't be a dope," said Wert. "I have."

What a lovely day that was.

It was the next morning on deck, lying somnolent, sunbathed and contented, that I was suddenly assailed by an odor so putrescent and overwhelming that I choked. Sitting upright, I looked beyond Wert to the barred entry that led downwards to below the water line of the ship. I don't know whether I said or only thought, after a second of fright, that the garbage unit must have blown a gasket.

Wert said in a very soft, tightly contained growl: "Pick up your blanket, Lael, and follow me down to the cabin. Close behind me. Something has happened."

I still could scarcely connect the smell with a human being.

Wert was getting slowly and carefully to his feet, holding his blanket in front of him. Obedient, I took mine and stood behind him. It occurred to me then that his bowels might have let loose, but even a latrine when the GIs had what they called the GIs, wartime diarrhea, did not smell like this.

"Walk behind me, down the stairs," said Wert quietly. "Cover me if you see anything."

In our procession to the cabin, we only passed one person. I remember her startled and frightened expression as she smelled the smell and her look around to see what in the world had happened. Wert moved quickly on past her, hugging the wall of the stairs, and I followed him. I saw that something was dripping at the bottom of his trousers and splashing onto his shoes.

"Quick," said Wert.

He unlocked the cabin door. I closed it behind us and he said, "Lock it," and I did. He went straight into the bathroom and I followed him. In a minute I was kneeling to help him off with his trousers. I gave thanks for a very strong stomach and head, or I should have failed him by being sick or fainting from the smell.

"Go away," said Wert. "Get out. This is unbearable."

"Lift your foot," I said.

We were whispering.

As his soaked gray-pink flannel trousers came off, and his underpants, we saw that blood, pus, and what seemed like fecal matter were streaming from a burst place in the scar.

"Go out! Go away!" said Wert urgently. "Leave me alone! I can't put you through this!"

"It's unimportant," I said.

It was my being spared anything, the sight and smell of any physical horror which he must go through because it had happened to him, that had become unimportant. The shock and revulsion we both felt was now shared and we acted simply and almost automatically, no longer speaking in whispers, but in low, almost ordinary voices.

He asked me to turn on the shower, good and hot. I did. I asked him if he needed anything, if he was in pain. He said he was not. Neither of us knew what had happened. The material was still flowing from his abdomen, but the amount was lessening.

While he showered, scrubbing himself down with soap, I turned the temperature all the way down to try to chill and clear away the thick, deadly smell that filled the cabin. I tried to open the porthole, but it was sealed shut to protect the air-conditioning system. Wert's trousers, underpants, socks and shoes I bundled into a heavy paper bag that had lined the wastebasket. I emptied a tin locker of two coats that hung in it, covered the ventilating holes with cardboard, and stuffed the bundle into the locker, closing the door tight. I had removed the belt, a woven Spanish leather one he liked, from the trousers, looking first to see if it were stained, thinking afterwards how odd it was you thought to do such things with part of your mind. His yellow turtleneck sweater had only a small stain, and I put it to soak in the basin.

"Get some ice from Henry, but don't let him in," said Wert from the shower. So I rang for Henry.

When Wert came out of the shower, I helped him dry himself and get into pajamas and dressing gown while he held two hand towels with some Kleenex to his now more slowly flowing wound. He wavered heavily on his feet and I helped him to the chair.

"The first thing to do is sit still and think," said Wert. He was very quiet and a little rigid in the chair. One hand he kept on the dressing gown, over the wound, to hold the dressing in place. With the other he twirled the bottle I had put in the ice bucket beside his chair.

The cabin had cleared a good deal and we could breathe in what was left of the odor or the clinging memory of it. The bath towels he had used were in the shower, with the hot water turned full on. The sweater was in a fresh basin of suds and water. I turned the heat up a little. The chimes had rung for lunch and after a brief bustle outside in the corridor our part of the ship was absolutely quiet. I opened the bottle of champagne and the cork popped loud in the stillness. The glasses I had iced were ready and the champagne sizzled into them.

"Chairs," said Wert, a mispronunciation of Chris's at three years old for "cheers," and we touched glasses. "If you can take it . . . I'd like more than anything else to be left alone with you. But there's still a lot of pressure, although I'm in less pain than I've been in at all, and I feel as if I might crack on open. That would be messy."

At a bullfight we had once seen a man ripped in the abdomen get up, holding himself together, and walk across the ring. Wert was offering to let me call in the doctor if I was afraid. At that moment I was not afraid of anything in the world, and neither was he. Fear, for the moment, was finished with.

There was nothing heroic in our decision to go on dealing with this unforeseen manifestation by the octopus blindly and alone. We were not, either, quixotically choosing to thus treat a man this way who might be made well by proper attention, but a man who might die a little sooner for lack of it. If Wert wanted to be left alone, for any reasons, including the crotchets of his attitude toward being tended, that was well with me. If he were to die that day, it might be peaceably, alone with me, and that was also well. If we could not cope, later on, we could holler—or not. We were not heroic in the face of the inevitable. We were still making free, individual choices.

We drank, pooh-pooh for doctors, hoo-ray for us, and to the Herseys for their superb memorial Bollinger 1947. Wert commanded me to eat, and I swallowed my reluctance and consulted Henry through the crack in the door I had chained. Henry knew that Wert was recovering from a serious operation and he had both a professional and a personal desire to please us. I told him we had had a little trouble, but did not want the medical department pestering us, and that he was to steal some bandages and adhesive tape, and to bring a sandwich for me, and I allied him to us in the traditional way with an outsize tip.

Henry came back with a small square of gauze and two tiny strips of tape. They would hardly have served for a cut finger. That was all he could get without an examination by the nurse or the doctor into the need for supplies. So later I went up to the ship shop and bought three boxes of Kotex and, since there were oddly enough none for sale, I borrowed four big safety pins from an army wife who had a baby aboard. With nail scissors I scalloped a clean bath towel down the middle and we bandaged Wert, pinning the split bath towel around the compress of four Kotex.

He did not want me to help him because of the still hideous smell and sight of the discharge . . . stay away, he said . . . but he was almost too weak to stand.

"How are the mighty fallen!" he said, as he took the Kotex with fastidious dislike for using it, laughing at himself ruefully because this detail seemed such a degradation. I was irrationally sorry he had to use it, but there was no absorbent cotton on sale, either, and at least, I said, Kotex was reasonably sanitary and deodorant. When I put the hand towels and paper handkerchiefs he had used over the wound in the locker with the other things, I realized as I opened the locker door that I must get these things overboard as soon as it was dark.

Settled and aired again, we realized that Wert might well be dying. I think he came close. The swellings went down but as they did so his feet, ankles, and legs grew as cold as death. We could not find his pulse and his breathing was very queer. A heavy, icy sweat came out on his forehead continually and now and then he wiped it away. His face grew very cold to the touch and very, very white. That afternoon a second hole opened above the first one, where another stitch had been. Wert remarked this quietly, and that his thighs were getting as cold as his ankles.

The sun wheeled over and set. He sat there, as I have seen beautiful old men sit in Spain, in dignity within the shells of their bodies. His hands, which were small, graceful, strong hands, were open and lay on his knees, wholly relaxed, except when he lifted one to wipe his forehead. He looked very peaceful and his face was thin, the skin transparent, and the outline of his bones very pure.

"I feel in a state of grace," he said.

9

We were on our way straight home, now, for after he lived through the night we felt that Wert would get to Ciboure, but that we could not go on to Naples.

I canceled the arrangements with the purser, and asked instead for a cable to be sent to the Export Line offices in Cannes for a wheel chair and attendant to meet us on the tender that would take us in to the dock. I wired also for a hotel room there, at the Carleton preferably, where we had stayed briefly during the war as guests of the U.S. Army when Cannes was a rest center for American officers and all war correspondents rated as "assimilated captains." The twenty-hour trip across the Pyrenees in a wandering train that constantly "arrested itself" and was without *wagonlit* cars for sleeping or a *wagon-restaurant* no longer seemed inviting, but there was no other convenient way to get home. It was more comfortable than the Central of Georgia and somewhat cleaner, but was apt to be crowded with customers and short on porters. The Mediterranean weather should be much warmer than our own on the Basque coast, and we could rest in Cannes a few days if need be.

The three days after Wert, as he wrote in his *carnet,* "blew hole" we stayed in the cabin. No one but Henry ministered to us, at our request. Henry made no comment on whatever he thought was happening. He cleaned the cabin swiftly whenever we asked him to, carried in a sturdier table so that we could eat our meals comfortably and served them himself, brought me a stack of extra-heavy paper bags so that I could dispose of whatever I wished so to dispose of. I went up once each morning for a five-minute turn around the deck at Wert's insistence. Every night, between sunset and broad moonlight, I took my paper bags, sneaked up the stairs and out to the bow and threw the bundle overboard when I hoped no one was looking, taking care that it went into the sea and not onto a lower deck. Only that first night, when I got rid of the clothes, was the odor so powerful that my package attracted distant attention.

Once I went to see the ship's doctor, on some pretext, to try to find out from him how to translate grains into milligrams. We wanted to know this because the bulletin we had about morphine was written with the references in milligrams and the supply we had was in quarter grains. To translate one into the other proved to be mathematically tricky, and it seemed you must know the substance you were translating as the equivalents differed. Since I could not tell the doctor it was morphine that interested me, Wert and I figured it out ourselves, not too inaccurately as it turned out.

"The hole is my friend," Wert said, the day after he blew it. "It's good for me."

We were absurd, discussing what in the world had happened, and it was not until we reached Cannes that the proper explanation occurred to either of us. Meantime we talked of words we had heard somewhere—of cancer "polyps" and "sloughing"—and speculated that the enemy, the octopus, had had polyps and was sloughing. Whatever had happened, the bursting relieved pressure from inside, reducing his pain to almost none. After the first night, when I had remade my bed so that I was lying the opposite way from him and could watch his face most of the night, Wert began to recover little by little.

As the second hole slowly closed, Wert no longer felt so

fragile and in danger of splitting open. He grew more fastidious than ever about my helping him to change our improvised bandages, but he was too weak to manage alone. "Keep your head turned and don't look and *don't* smell. Christ, how I hate smelling bad!" he said. I could assure him by next day that he could not be so much as sniffed, once thickly covered and bound.

Although he felt better than he had at all, his physical weakness was very great. Shaving and showering wore him out and when he moved about the cabin it was from hand hold to hand hold. He tried to write a few notes to friends and family, but gave up because his hand was not steady and to write anything tired him outrageously. To me he dictated a short list of cables I was to send one day, and gave me messages for people, especially for his son, Bill, for whose sake he so regretted not having one more year. He wanted Bill to know the pride he took in him, the high hopes he held for him, the rewarding sense of his older son's manhood he had felt during their last weekend together. Our children would have the knowledge, the emotional confidence, and the stable memories of their undivided lifetimes with us both, young as they were and short as the time had been.

For his amusement, Wert experimented mildly with morphine, which acted like a drug when it was not provided with pain, its antidote. Melting a quarter grain in a teaspoon of warm water, he gave himself a shot of it and noted the results: immediate slight haziness; five minutes later, groggy, blackish, dry mouth, sweat . . . and a certain brief, light-headed gaiety during which he was full of charm and very entertaining and which he enjoyed. But not sufficiently, he said, to take up drugs even now, even out of curiosity, when he would scarcely have time to become an addict. He liked being wholly himself better.

For all I had discussed literature with Wert so often in twelve years, there was still so much he had to say about books and writing that was penetrating, provocative, and exciting that I wish I had taken notes. I'm afraid I should only garble any attempt to recapture his random, ranging comment. Besides, I talked, too, and our conversations were full of old assumptions and agreements, as well as his fresh reconsiderations and evaluations. Wert had read everything, or read at everything, translated into or written in the English language he so loved and admired. In the last few years he had given up trying to read any author who did not deeply please him, and thus, for instance, had left Proust reluctantly to others, and had reread, in the past winter's orgy of reading, all of Stendhal and Melville. But I cannot hope to do him justice. It had taken him all his years to formulate his personal, not final, judgments on writing and he would have had to write his own essay on it . . . I could never make notes except in detachment, and I was too greedily with him and enjoying him to try to preserve anything he said except disconnected sentences which stayed in my memory and the larger feeling of his love of writing and the writing man's search for truth. Next to living, he loved the writing about it best.

One morning, when he was talking about Fitzgerald, I found myself not crying but without warning soaked in my own streaming tears.

"Cry if you need to, dear love," Wert said—a most intolerant man of tears—with such compassion, "while I'm around to comfort you."

"I don't want you to die! I don't want you to die!" I cried out, and he said, "I wouldn't trade places with you."

Another time, he said, "You must tell Johnny Hersey everything that happens, just as it happens, bad and good. Write it or say it. Because I find it is to Johnny I am saying goodbye. Through Johnny to men, to all good men."

I did not need to remember what he said about books for Johnny, for they had talked long and well together about writing.

By Friday, Wert was in pain again, and went back to moderate doses of dolophine, and now we were anxious to get back to Ciboure before any new trouble could develop. Besides, the ship had become vaguely hostile and the cabin confining.

The hostility was to mystery. Children cabined on our corridor tried to peer in at us. Several people had spoken to me inquisitively during my few minutes on deck. The dining steward waylaid me and wanted to know why we ate—full meals—in our cabin. The purser was curious. I offered no explanation beyond the vaguest, not wanting to involve myself in lies or even in conversation. The afternoon before the ship was due in Gibraltar there was an angry banging at the door.

When I went to answer, a nurse was there in uniform. I had seen her twice before, once when I went to the doctor's office on my trumped-up visit, the second time in the corridor, where she had asked me rudely why Henry had wanted a bandage for us and I had replied that it was nothing at all and to let us alone. This time she came in, pushing past me and staring at Wert, who was sitting in his chair drinking his afternoon champagne.

"What's all this about a wheel chair?" she demanded belligerently. "We have already sent in our reports to port authorities that we have no disease on board. What's the matter with you? Why didn't you report to us? We have to know!"

She behaved as though Wert were concealing leprosy.

Wert said, offhand and quiet, "I have cancer."

"Oh," she said. "Oh. Oh." Then she got very flustered and apologetic. She kept saying, "You know how it is," and we kept saying we did. Finally she backed out, as relieved to go as we were to have her go.

"*Nuts!*" said Wert.

The water roughened as we came first within the effect and then within sight of land. As we moved into the Straits we could see Africa on one side and Spain on the other.

The past February, trying to circumvent February's annual depression, we had stopped trying to work early in the month and gone to Africa. It was bright weather the day we left Ciboure, and the children had leaned far out of the windows and waved at us leaving in the car. It was warm in southern Spain, but by the time we reached Casablanca, it was snowing. The cold spell was the "worst within living memory" and certain roads we wanted to take were blocked by rare, heavy snows. The country depressed us. Both Spanish and French Morocco had standards of poverty lower even than those in tragically poor Andalusia. The hatred of Arab for European was a still thing, then. The only eruptions of it had been temporary and sporadic, but we had felt it, on the roads, on the streets and even in the tourist hotels. Until we got as far as Marrakech we had been depressed at being in Africa, almost sorry that we had not stayed at home instead of going to distract ourselves with the feel and look of a new piece of world. In Marrakech we yielded as ever to physical enchantment. It was beautiful and while we were there spring came. February ended and it was March. By the time we set sail again for Algeciras on our way home, sailing on the ferry from Ceuta instead of from Tangiers, he had fallen in love with me in the spring and it was the most glowing of all our springs.

There had been a rainbow over Gibraltar and we had stood on the deck of that ferry, looking at it with wonder and holding hands. Wert said to me, wonderingly, "What's wrong with this? It's too perfect."

In April, in Ciboure, he had written a note describing this scene, torn it across, and then saved it. He had written: "Speaking of wonders, there was the rainbow over Gibraltar. We were crossing from Ceuta to Algeciras, about a month ago, and the weather in North Africa that morning had been sunny and warm. But we could see that it was raining in Spain, in the mountains above Algeciras to the left, and there seemed to be a squall around Gibraltar, on the right. A few minutes after the ferry left Ceuta, while we were still in the shelter of the African mountains, the base of the rainbow appeared, springing out of Gibraltar itself, leaving the rock to be seen through all its colors. For quite a while it was only a short arc, but then it began to grow, reaching up and then over and finally down toward the Spanish mountains; it must have taken it half an hour to touch down its farther end. It moved a little, too, as we did, so that Gibraltar was within its compass, and all the bay between there and Algeciras, and the white town itself when it began to appear, and the mountains to the west. It was really a double rainbow, running the spectrum through twice, and it was the largest and most perfect I had ever seen. Ships sailed into it, and were dream ships, and sailed out on the farther side. By now we were more than halfway across the Straits and coming into the rain, and as we entered it and the boat began to pitch a little the ends of the rainbows curved toward us and we were in it, too. One end melted away beside the boat, but the other actually came down into the bow and we could see the bow through it. But it was far away as well as near, there and here at the same time, and as we neared land it began to fade. I tried to think of a story that would make use of it, a man at the height of his happiness, deep, firm happiness made with a woman, knowing that such happiness must end, wanting the end of himself before that day—but the story wouldn't end."

There was a single rainbow now over the rock of Gibraltar when our ship *S.S. Constitution* came to slow, swaying rest in the Straits. It was November 12th. I helped Wert to the porthole and we stood together looking out from the cabin. It was a slender rainbow, pale in its colors.

We knew now that the cancer must have already been there, within him, on that spring day when we sailed between Ceuta and Algeciras. We knew now that the biggest of the white ships we had seen through the rainbow in March was the ship we were on today, for I had checked the date and the hour. We knew the end of the story now, and we were glad it had not ended, in perfection, in the spring. There is another note to himself, on a scrap of paper, among the few notes he left for his tentatively titled *Sixty Days in a Lifetime:* "Hit hard on swim refusal—I'd have drowned the best part of my life."

10

The ship's wheel chair was a lightweight, shining, nickel-and-leather affair. Henry wheeled it and a young officer escorted us a labyrinthine way down to the place where the side of the ship had been opened to permit the passengers for Cannes to disembark onto a small open ferry. The gangway was cleared. Up it came two burly Frenchmen with a wooden litter complete with mattress, blankets, and pillow. It had double handles at each end and a backrest which was raised and propped up by wooden slats. The two men handled the awkward and weighty contraption casually, with coordinated, swaying movements.

Wert's chief worry was that his amateur bandage might slip. He made the transfer from chair to litter with caution, impeded by everybody's help. Once installed, he said cheerfully that he felt like an ass, but would be comfortable, provided he was not inadvertently dropped. The men negotiated the steep, precarious descent to the ferry's deck and then, with some relief, set the litter down on its four wooden legs. The other passengers regarded us with momentary curiosity.

In the customs shed I was accommodated quickly, at the request of a girl who represented the Export Lines in Cannes. There was a wonderful fuss over whether a doll I had bought for Timberlake was an "important" doll, subject to duty. I claimed, playing the game, that it was not *un*important and the customs officer dismissed it as insufficiently important—not chic, too simply dressed. Several Christmas-wrapped gifts for the children were opened suspiciously, yielded inexpensive toys, and we were through, and our drugs were safe. It was a good moment. Wert was already needing a lot of dope again.

The men picked up Wert in the litter, trotted rhythmically with him to a converted station wagon into which the wooden bed fitted, with a chair beside it for me. We arrived thus, totally conspicuous, at the hotel which was not the Carleton, closed for these out-of-season months, but an old-fashioned hotel catering year around to the British. There was no one on the grounds, and Wert, embarrassed by the cumbersome trappings of his weakness, insisted on debarking in the graveled driveway and making his own way, slowly, with his cane, to the entrance. In a short while we were sitting in a bedroom in two armchairs in front of a big open bay window overlooking the Mediterranean and the sun was flooding our privacy.

Wert turned to me, with a slow grin, and said, "Good God, woman, it has just occurred to me what happened . . ."

"Of *course*," I said, simultaneously enlightened, and we began to laugh. We laughed like fools, and then subsided into small sounds of amusement at ourselves.

The explosion on the boat had been caused by an abscess. Whether it was an interior one or an exterior affair of the stitches we were never sure. The facts—that it had been the size of a melon, that he had quite nearly died, and that the experience with it was in no way altered by comprehension of its cause—did not diminish the simplicity of the explanation. Us and our polyps and sloughing! What we needed was a drain. Abscesses presumably healed and did not repeat themselves.

"So that should be over soon," I said.

"Let's get home," said Wert. "Let's go on tonight."

"Think you can make it?" I asked. He looked very gray and exhausted, though still lit by laughter.

"Certainly," said Wert, impatient. "Go get some decent material for bandages, and tickets for tonight." He wanted to get back to Ciboure to finish off this extraneous accident of his disease and to get to work while he still could.

I tried, but this was Saturday and there was no space at all on the only train. I even had difficulty getting two lower bunks in a compartment for six on the next night. This train carried a few such compartments—"*couchettes*," three tiers of bunks on which there were blankets and pillows where you could lie down in clothes or a dressing gown in whatever company you found yourself. Also, if we were lucky, we could find a compartment in which to sit for part of the night.

During the next day, with Wert neatly pinned into wide rubberized cloth bandages under which were sterile gauze pads, we took a slow ride in a horse carriage along the shore toward Juan-les-Pins. Wert called all flowers bougainvillaea unless they were roses, deriding his abysmal ignorance of horticultural nomenclature. The real ones he called bougainvillaea bougainvillaea and detested. For all his prejudice, we enjoyed the curtains of purple on the pastel houses, the November roses, the many other kinds of "bougainvillaea" growing beside the polished, park-like shore that had been converted wholly to the use and pleasure of tourists and vacationers, whether temporary, transient, or permanent. Nice place to *visit,* we agreed, smug because we would reach our own coast tomorrow.

I had telephoned Madame Sueur the afternoon before, waiting until the children were in school, Saturday being a school day in France and Thursday the free weekday. Ama considered the long-distance telephone a serious extravagance to be used with all the economy of the old ten-word telegram and asked few questions, barely containing her impatience when my instructions seemed wordy. The children were well. She awaited us eagerly. Yes, she would transfer us into Chris's small bedroom with the southern exposure, which was the only one we could hope to heat, moving in a narrow bed for me to supplement the other one in which Chris now slept. She would build a fire in the living room. Yes (laughing), she had swept and scrubbed and waxed the bottom of the fireplace, but she had learned our curious, alien ways by *this* time and she had enough ashes kept in a box to make an ash-bed for the fire before we came back. The children were to be sent on to school Monday afternoon as usual, for I did not want them to see Pop until he had rested a bit. No, he did not look well. We had had trouble on the ship. Ama cut me off tactfully. He was all right, of course, naturally, he was all right. It was a question of time. She would have a strong man meet us at the station with a car. Au 'voir.

"Ama doesn't want to know. I don't think I can tell her," I had said to Wert.

He had shrugged. All either of us wanted was our own kind of emotional peace, whether it was based on knowledge and acceptance or on ignorance on the part of others.

When we got on the train at 21:20 hours a Swiss from Geneva was standing outside the compartment where we had our space, dressing gown over his trousers, his white shirt unbuttoned at the neck. With that polite but unalterable determination of the Swiss, he tried to put us straight to bed. While I was having the luggage hoisted onto the racks above the tiers of bunks and was trying to arrange with the porter-conductor to let us sit awhile in the empty compartment of seats next door, he was arguing indefatigably. We should *not* sit up awhile, he said. We had no *right* to occupy seats in the next compartment, empty or not. We had *paid* for, and reserved, the two lower bunks, indeed the *best* bunks, in the *couchette* with him. It was our duty and according to the regulations for us to lie down in them. It was, of course, a little early for sleeping if one was not accustomed to going to bed before 9:30, but this was irrelevant. One did what one contracted to do. He himself who rarely elongated himself before eleven nevertheless would do so and we must follow his example. It would simplify everything. The porter had no *right* to allow us to sit in additional seats for which we had not paid.

Wert dealt with the self-righteous Swiss quite simply by turning off his comprehension of French, which he could do at will. I carried on a *sotto voce* conversation with the train man, both of us politely ignoring the increasingly exasperated attacks of the Swiss. The porter said of course my husband and I could sit in unoccupied seats as long as possible, but the train had been running regrettably full. I pressed into his hand a thousand francs, which he seriously tried to return, saying he was not in the least sure he could keep the extra seats, or preferably the next-door compartment itself, free for us. I said to accept my gift and do what he could.

The Swiss went into the *couchette* and slid shut the door with a bang. Wert had already taken a corner seat in the compartment and was pouring himself some hot tea from a thermos I had brought along. The porter wished us good luck. The fortune of the night was uncertain, but we agreed that the porter would, as the French did, break his neck to earn his *pourboire* now that he had retained it. We would be left in as much peace as his ingenuity and the traffic would permit.

Wert said, "You're the only woman in the world who could tip for me." It was a compliment I cherished then and still cherish inordinately.

By 3:00 A.M., the porter had successfully diverted all customers to other seats in other compartments, and at last I went in to try to sleep a little while in the bunk. The Swiss was snoring like Dominique's grandfather Toyos, about whom the whole neighborhood complained. The train clattered and whistled to one of its brief, innumerable stops and another man came in, climbed into the bunk over mine, went instantly to sleep and began to snore antiphonally with the Swiss. I went back to Wert, who was feeling too uncomfortable to try to lie down. We opened the package containing tomorrow's breakfast and lunch and two bottles of wine and had a 4:00 A.M. snack. Later we changed Wert's bandages in the filthy toilet at the end of the car.

By afternoon Monday, when the incessant stopping was at the stations of the charming, familiar villages in the Basque country, I was even more grateful than glad we were there. The Swiss, although he had slept undisturbed, was still indignant at our incorrect behavior. He did not speak when I went in to the *couchette,* now converted for daytime, and began to haul the bags down from the rack ready to hoist them out the window at the St. Jean-de-Luz station. My struggles softened him finally, and as we drew into the station at Guéthary, the red-tile-roofed Basque village before our own, he unfolded his arms and condescended to explain to me where we were.

"I know this country well," I said.

"How can you? You are an American!" he said, refolding his arms.

There was no reply to this. He looked piqued when I hailed the welcome bulk of Ttottette Tollechea out the window . . . I don't know whether because I was disobeying the sign which said not to lean out the window or because I knew somebody. Ttottette had come to meet us, as he was a trucker and all the fishermen were at sea that day.

"*Agur,* Ttottette!" I yelled, and began handing out the bags, working fast for the train pulled in and out quickly and more than once passengers and baggage for St. Jean-de-Luz had gone on, haplessly, to Hendaye. Wert, as agreed, was independently making his slow way off the car. I ran down the corridor and dropped off beside him with a second to spare. He was laughing at me and the Swiss, and we were home.

"It's good to live in a place you are always glad to get back to," said Wert, looking at the harbor, where only three or four of the bright boats lay at anchor, looking at the skyline of grave and graceful mountains, at the waves of a high tide washing in white over the gray stone breakwater into the green bay, at the sweet shapes of the houses, trimmed in dark green, blue or red, that fronted the quai.

Ama and Gashousha Toyos stood at our gate to greet us, smiling as they always did upon our homecomings. "How handsome they are," said Wert as we moved toward the fine-bodied, black-haired women who were our landlady and neighbor, our household staff, and our friends. We embraced them and went in through the small, white-walled rooms of the house, over the dark floors deeply waxed to velvet, and out onto the terrace. Our rhythm was immediately the slower rhythm of Europe, the still slower rhythm of the village.

We stood on the terrace, warmed by an oblique, late-afternoon, last-of-late-summer sun. The terrace faced south and overlooked the back of Ciboure and its tiny "suburb," Kechiloa. Urrugne, a span of bright white walls and red-tiled roofs with gray-towered church and sand-colored *pelote* court, crested a green hill, lower than our own, in the middle distance. The bare-topped Basses-Pyrénées ambled down toward the sea across our far horizons, La Rhune the peak from which they descended. *La Rhune, Irun, Urrugne*—we could never sound the native distinctions between one kind of *u* and another.

The terrace was protected from all winds except the south wind by the thick, hundred-and-fifty-year-old walls of the house within which it had been set. Even in winter, when to sit inside meant huddling by the fire in layers of clothing, we could bare our arms and strip our sweaters and stretch our bared legs out there in a noontime sun. It had been a narrow balcony when we first moved in, but Ama had enlarged it for our pleasure when we returned from the United States to Ciboure again. Enlisting her sons, who were fishing-boat engineers, she had directed the extension of the cement floor to twice its breadth and the reinstallation of the balcony rail at the new edge. Worrying over the strength of it, she had constantly badgered her amateur masons.

"Ama!" I remembered son Maurice saying to her in exasperation. *"Ecoute!* We are making it strong enough for Monsieur *and* Madame *and* the table *and* the bottle *and* the glass. He will NOT one day tumble into the garden."

Leaving the terrace, we strolled back in through the living room, where the fire was burning above its bed of hoarded ashes, and up the polished, dark stairs to the bathroom to wash off the train dirt and change Wert's bandages, which were no longer insecure since we had proper materials. I called over the banister for tea on the terrace. We would come in when the sun set and be there, by the fire, when the children came in from school. Everything had become simple and effortless.

As we went down, Ama and Gashousha in the kitchen were telling each other how well Wert looked. *"Dites!"* said Ama. "After an operation so grave." They raised their voices to be overheard, to be sure we knew that they were repeating to each other what they had said to us.

We sat on the terrace over tea and made old-favorite, well-worn remarks to each other. The view, we said, which was motionless, composed of villages, trees, fields, hillsides and mountains, changed so much more, moment to moment, day to day, weather to weather, than the view from the tower over the restless bay and violent ocean. Was it that we preferred, as in literature, the classic changes of quality to the romantic changes of shape? The cherry tree, we said, was losing its leaves early this year. There was no tree house in it, we remarked, and perhaps our children had outgrown them and we were getting older than we thought.

We remembered a succession of tree houses that Chris and Begnat Toyos had built, the first one when they were five. Chris had come running in to get us. "Oh, *POEL!*" he had said. "Begnat and me have built a *cabane* in the *arbre*. We've got EVERYTHING except a floor, some *murs,* and a top."

We had gone out with him, curious to see a house that had everything except a floor, some walls, and a roof. In the tree the boys had installed a broken stool and a small wooden table and on the table a pot full of flowers.

We spoke and thought of other homecomings.

"What is there about those women at the gate that makes you remember so much and feel so good?" asked Wert.

"They make me feel like the bride the sun shone on," I said, remembering the time we had come home together from the station after we had been separated from each other for a month. They had followed us in then, and seen us up the stairs. There was no slyness in their seeing us up, no embarrassment, not even vicarious pleasure, no judgment or censorship, only benevolence.

"Blessed," said Wert, also remembering.

"Undemanding," I said. "Recurrent."

"Self-contained," said Wert, "and whole." He added, "It's not just us. Remember how the children reacted when they saw those women again."

They had been there, smiling like that, when we had all returned after two and a half years away. The children had been nervous and shy, feeling guilty, lonely, and forlorn as we approached Ciboure and they became sharply conscious of how much they had forgotten. Timberlake remembered the face of a Basque doll she had left behind, and the names of people, but she had forgotten the people and the language. Chris remembered the roads, streets, trees, and mountains, but not the language or the people, except to remember, not sure he still would, that he had loved them. The smiles had been the key to memory, and the children, after a suspended moment, had flown into the arms of the women. The "readjustment" we had figured would take a few weeks was over. It remained only for memory to recover in relearning the words of the language and for fresh affection to reaffirm and recapture the emotional memories of the old.

Still, memory alone tended to immobilize the fluid and to fix on the immobile and lose all movement and detail, I thought.

"I'll hate it if I only remember—in tableaux," I said to Wert, struck with fright at this.

"As long as you don't need to falsify or censor the tableaux," said Wert, "La-el, it'll be like this view. Still, not static. You can't possibly see it all at once, but each time you look at it you see it different without changing it."

"I'm afraid of forgetting or remembering selectively," I said, needing his help.

"You can forget as much as you please of something that's good enough," said Wert. "It's all there when you want it."

We were inside waiting for them when Chris and Timberlake ran in, preceded by their excited voices. After the blind-seeming, casual glances the young give to appearances, they seemed to find Pop unchanged. Chris spoke of renewing Pop's guitar lessons in the late afternoons and Timberlake brought her *cahier mensuel* to show how she was first in her class, after being second to one Marie José Oyarsabal the month before. They were pleased and rather surprised that we had brought them pre-Christmas homecoming presents.

The abruptly broken pattern of our family life was renewed within a few minutes, as if it were unchanged except by an ordinary trip away. By nightfall the shift of rooms in the little house seemed retroactive, so easily had we changed, so quickly settled, having habits of this. Chris had established his "laboratory" in the attic cupboard where I'd kept my papers and arranged his papers geometrically on the desk, cleared of my confusion, in what had been my third-floor workroom and was now his bedroom. Timberlake had tumbled her belongings into a tiny room up there and pinned a penciled *"Privé"* to the door. Our old double bedroom on the second floor was ready for any work I might do now, and across from it was the bedroom that had been Chris's, set up for us with an extra narrow bed so placed that I could open my eyes and look directly across at Wert's pillow. *Treasure*

Island, Tom Sawyer and *Les Trois Mousequetaires* beside Chris's old bed, now Wert's, had been replaced by Gibbon, Butler, and Montaigne.

The next morning there was shopping to do for Wert's comfort: another electric heater to supplement the one in the bathroom, small enough not to blow our fragile fuses; extra blankets, now that Wert and I no longer shared blankets and body warmth in a double bed; a giant thermos for hot tea through the night; a pot to sterilize things in; a grate so that we could burn coal as well as wood in the fireplace beside which he would now work until—and unless—he got well enough to walk up to the tower and to work there in isolation, beauty, and discomfort. The tower was exposed on four sides and heated only by a wood-burning *poêle,* fuel must be carried up the crooked narrow stairs; it leaked and was drafty.

That afternoon I went to see Dr. Cartier in his office to tell him before he came to see Wert the news I knew would shock him deeply.

His handsome face, that of a man who was at once aesthete and ascetic, expressed chagrin, personal sorrow, and a moment of grim revolt against medical facts which left him helpless. Then it fell into old, well-marked lines of sympathy, professional interest, regret, and medical acceptance. When I told him Wert knew, his eyebrows leaped up and his face darkened.

"Why does he know?" he asked. "How?"

"Because I told him!"

He lifted his arms, the shoulders tilting inward, the elbows spreading slightly, the hands with the palms curved upward, in the Frenchman's vivid body-expression of amazement, powerlessness, resignation, and acknowledgment that there were not only two but many sides to every question. He would come to the house at six.

The cavity of the abscess was profound. Cartier was worried about the intestinal wall. As he probed, expounded, and then installed the drain, explaining to me how to sterilize and reinstall it in the morning, how to pour in the antiseptic, I was glad the experience on the ship had given me a kind of immunity to my own squeamishness. I could do anything for Wert so long as I did not have to hurt him. Almost anyone learns to do what he must, but I was pleased to have been shocked out of certain reactions which would, at this point, have irked the doctor and which Wert would have had to humor. Dr. Cartier scolded both of us for not calling in the doctor on the ship. Nothing could make him understand that, nor did we try. We were not in the least sorry, and our apologies for our foolhardiness were perfunctory and unmeant.

As he took leave of me at the door, Cartier said, "I do not understand why there was no operation at all, Madame, in the United States. Here we would have removed some of . . . but . . ." He shrugged, and then added as if to himself, *"Madame, un homme magnifique!"*

Wert was able to go off dope for the rest of the week. The abscess was healing and its cavity contracting. He slept well, relaxing in the heavier air after the stimulation of the American continent.

It pleased him most when he found he could work in the mornings, working slowly, but against time, on *Sixty Days in a Lifetime.* He completed the outline, noting that the *Octopus* section, the story of his cancer, should be broken in half "perhaps where reflection comes in, then: which are the two points of my life worth recalling. . . ." He made no notes for *A Virginia Childhood,* planning to leave the writing of this section until last. *A Rainbow on Gibraltar* would be hardest, he thought, the story of his life and *hubris* "with corny ending. And yet it was the true ending; I could not have made it up; and so I'll tell it as it was."

We had never written about each other—that is, we had never used each other as the models or the basis for any fictional characters. We did not want to affect or change or touch or fix or finish off, by writing about it, any part of our relationship. We had not finished with anything about each other. I could claim never to have used myself fictionally, and Wert could claim to have used himself only as partial model, but that was quibbling. You use yourself whatever you write. When I knew that he was writing also about me, I knew how certain he was that nothing could be changed, now, because it was ending. "It's going to be the devil for me to try to describe you as I see you," he complained one night, when I moved restlessly, aware that his stare was an artist's impersonal stare. He never got around to trying, and I am glad.

In planning to tell of "the search for the essence of perfection in this marriage," he talked to me about certain incidents—the day, for instance, when after a wretched, disharmonious misunderstanding we had found harmony and delight again over lunch and had walked up the quai in Paris from the Peregordine afterwards talking about *hubris* and how we defined for ourselves this word: man defying his fate, even the laws of the gods or God, and taking violent and dangerous pride in himself. Pepe, the *Time* and *Life* chauffeur, had seen us, which we did not know at the time, and had said afterwards to us more than once, "I do not forget it. It was better than young lovers."

I I

We settled down perhaps too quickly and naturally into what was a modified form of normal wintertime life in Ciboure. Our attitudes lost some of their sensitive intensity. It seemed to us, and we could not help listening to Cartier, who was deliberately encouraging, as if we might have a winter, a spring, even a summer, even a year. You can't be intense or even aware of the presence of death for a year.

To surround Wert with peace so that he could work was the biggest practical problem. In Sneden's Landing, where our beloved and absurd dwelling had been economically evolved out of a stable sixty feet square and three and a half stories high, we had the luxury of space to waste for purposes of isolation. His tower in Bordagain had been a signal tower, isolated of itself, and his workroom was the old signal room on top of it. It was not easy to insulate the living room in our tiny house, surrounded by a compact garden, where two Basque women—and the Basques are only laconic with strangers—two children, their friends, who all seemed to prefer ours to their own houses, and I, lived our active, talkative lives. To the rallying murmur of "Pop's working," we managed. All minors went straight from kitchen to third floor if it was raining and stayed in the tree and courtyard out front if it was not. The boys played *pelote* against the front wall of the house, endangering the dining-room window instead of the living room's. The girls gathered and gossiped and played and knitted on the bench out front instead of under the cherry trees in back. Ama and Gashousha carried on their endless duologue over the laundry tubs in the "garage," doing laundry in the mornings for the first time in their lives, during the time while Wert was sitting downstairs with the long yellow pad attached to the leather lap board Marion Ascoli had sent him for shipboard, a pot of sharpened pencils beside him. This was an enormous concession, but I pointed out to Ama that she herself would scrub a house, whitewash walls, launder linen sheets in cement floor-tubs, weed a garden and walk ten miles with a child on her back, rather than write a letter of two paragraphs. I told her it was almost as hard for a writer to write two paragraphs he cared about. She laughed, disbelieving—if so, who would be fool enough to write for a living? Nevertheless she gave over her lifetime routine.

I worked a little, upstairs, while he was working down. I did not feel like doing any writing of my own, chiefly because I did not want to separate myself by that much from Wert just then. There was one piece of work Wert had already done and would have liked to have time to re-do that meant more to us both at this time than any other, since one man's courage was bolster for every man's. I worked at cutting this article, written in 1950, on Woop, the cartoonist. Woop was a man who had confirmed his life and his belief in himself and in mankind not by the manner of his dying but in the face of death. Although Woop had felt, himself, that the days of his importance, his identity with history, were over, Wert had considered that such a man was always important to know about, to have known. It had been difficult to put his subject into any magazine formula, for publication. Whenever he had tried to revise it himself, Wert had complained that he only wanted to make it longer instead of shorter as it needed to be. I tried for him, without changing a word, or distorting by selection, to choose and fit together a description and some of the things Woop had said to Wert. If it meant so much to me, it would, I thought, to others. I also wrote a rough ending for the *Estudiantina* article for him to comment on and edit, since he had no time to finish it himself.

The pages of Wert's *carnet* during the week were marked "Better," "Not so good," "More better," "Some better," and, every day, "A little work."

We took the weekend "off." Saturday we drove to Ascain, five miles away, to walk around its square and to lunch on a bird and a bottle. Sunday we went to Biriatou, on the border, and looked across the Bidasoa River into Spain while Maigy Hirribarren served us *piperade* and welcomed us with gaiety and old established affection, the look behind her eyes recognizing death, for her brother was also dying, of old wounds from two wars. I began to learn to drive as if my tires were bare feet, for Wert was very tender and a jolt caused him to turn white. But he felt "fine," as Sunday night ended our first week back at home.

It is hard to remember in peacetime how you longed for it during the war. On Monday morning, when Wert woke up with "gripes, constipation, gas," he took umbrage at his condition and became a very sick man.

Demanding that Cartier come up daily, he deferred almost obsessively to the doctor's efforts on his behalf. He kept dope down and homelier medications up, so that bowels would move and gas disperse. He dieted. It was hard to tell when and whether he was being stern with himself or indulgent when the gas pains distressed him. Lord knows it was bad enough at times, even then. Gas is peculiarly difficult to handle because deadening the pain also stops the outlets and increases what you must deaden. It became a hideous problem later. At this time he was nervy, truculent, complaining, and brave, and I could not tell how bad it was and was wrenched with pity for him and to assuage my pity bustled and tended him.

There is no question that writing places a physical strain on the guts, on the intestines. I don't pretend to explain this. It's so. Wert continued to work, doggedly, irritably, working on the section about his childhood because it was easier. The pages were weary-sounding and lifeless when I read them later. He knew these pages were not worth any price, and yet he would not stop, and the very price he paid to write them made them precious to him.

It was not a time when he could have or would have committed suicide. He did not like himself well enough. To die would have been a defeat, a negation. Yet what he was going through was very bad and promised worse and frightened him. His love for me for the moment was that of his dependence on me.

I became wife-nurse to my patient and it was what he wanted then. It was easier, much so, than his demand for a companionship that called for the best I had to give. I was by turns ingratiating and bossy, exuding the sympathy I felt and summoning it when I did not. I asked the doctor all those questions to which the answers, if the doctor is scrupulously honest, as Cartier was, are questions.

"I'm living in my messy guts," said Wert, momentarily disgusted on one of these days. "Aren't you bored, talking about them?"

"Mostly no," I said, and I wasn't.

The ways and absorptions of invalidism have anesthetic qualities and a welcome mediocrity and they are so very excusable. We humored his moods, as we had always humored his moods; met his demands, as we had always met his demands, now the trivial demands of his sickness. We felt pity and honored his self-pity. Doctor was content and relieved to have a normal relationship with a very ill man who would do what he told him to, which was the best he knew to tell him. Children and Basque women accepted a sick man in the house as a limited liability and went their own ways otherwise. "Not with a bang, but a whimper . . ."

The most emphatic note in his *carnet* that week, among a run of such notes as "Bad Appetite" and "Gripes," is "SHAT."

That Sunday night, at the end of our second week at home,

Wert had the first *crise,* a reaction of the nerve ends which causes the pain for which this kind of cancer is justly infamous.

Monday he did not try to work. We sat together, fought through the second *crise* that came about four o'clock, fighting the terrifying seizure with dolophine again, and talked hard all day.

"What a temptation," he said. "You let 'it' and 'them' take over. You give in. 'It's' responsible for killing you and 'they're' responsible for taking care of you, so you get aggrieved. I'd be going to a hospital for 'terminal care' next. Why not? Why take any responsibility yourself? But if I'd been a different kind of man I'd have been in 'their' hands already a couple of years ago and maybe I'd have saved my life. If I'd been a different kind of man I'd have had a different kind of life. I'll take the one I had and what's left of it. In the immortal words of Patrick Henry," he said, going gay, putting on the Southern-senator pose and voice he used when he amused himself by reciting this speech, all of which he knew by heart . . . (I still hear echoes of "resounding arms" and "Why stand we here idle?") . . . "'Give me libutty or give me death!' And I'll take you for wife not nurse."

We did not turn on the lights even when the dusky-dark of the early night filled the room, isolating the glow of the fire. This was the end of November and the days were very short in our latitude. It was five-fifteen when Chris came home from school, earlier than Timberlake, who had elected to stay daily for the post-school study hall open for those who preferred to do their homework there instead of carrying it home. Chris knocked on the door and we called him in. He blinked in the dusk and then peered closely at his father. His face brightened and he said, "Hey!" and stopped.

Then, "Hey, Pop," he said, "how about a guitar lesson? You've got *Sol y Sombra* next." Wert had promised Chris, when he started taking guitar lessons from his son in the summer, that when he, a lifetime frustrated guitar player, had mastered the gay *passe doble, Sol y Sombra,* he would buy his professor-son a new guitar, concert class, and take as his own Chris's ordinary guitar.

"Fifteen minutes, just to get started again," said Wert. "I need some new callouses on my finger ends. But I sure would admire to learn that piece."

When Timberlake came in from school, Chris went out to meet her. We heard his voice, joyous and boyish, in the hall. "Hey, Timberlake. Come QUICK and see Pop. He's *feeling* good."

Timberlake ran into the room, her stray lovelocks stirring like vine tendrils. "It's so nice," she said, flirting with sidelong glances, her real pleasure showing in the pinkening of her tinted face. "It's so very nice for a girl to have a Pop who is feeling good. I do like my Pop."

"You're an outrageous female," said Wert, reaching for her, his beautiful eyebrows mocking the game they made of their affection.

Later, after the children had gone cheerful to bed, I saw his face change. "I'm in for it again," he said.

I went to boil the hypodermic and needle, for a shot would act more quickly than pills. The *crise* was brief, but grim.

The next day, Tuesday, he noted in his *carnet:* "Better. Some work. Smaller crise." Across Monday's page he wrote large: "Last Sunday to Sunday. The week out. The week the octopus almost won, the week we almost lost each other. I had become a patient. Came back Sunday night with dolophine."

The notes ran on as the days went by and November ended and December began. "Feeling good." "Crise." "Fine (look out!)." "Crise lunchtime." "Better. Tired!" "Good night. Worked a little." "Awful. No fart for 2 days." "Better." "AWFUL CRISE." "Feeling fine." "Almost no sleep. Music. Work. It hurts like hell."

It was a record, not an absorption. The good hours were the best of a lifetime.

12

THE MAN THEY COULDN'T BREAK
By Charles Wertenbaker

If you saw him coming toward you—and if you knew of him only that he called himself Woop and was a famous cartoonist —you would think that with mordant humor he had made a walking cartoon of himself. He walked with the clumsy gait of a man embarrassed by his strength, and he could not stand less than six feet three or weigh less than 300 pounds, most of which was bone and muscle. The sleeves of his tan cotton shirt had been cut off above the elbow, then split to the shoulders for comfort; his arms were too large to hang straight down, and they made a kind of parenthesis enclosing a massive torso. But it was the face that summoned incredulous attention.

It was also massive, even on such a body, and in the center of it was a red, bulbous, wide-nostriled nose. From above the curve of the nostrils, somewhere in the vicinity of the cheekbones, began a coarse, reddish-brown mustache, an unbridled growth that swept over the entire mouth and reached almost to the chin. It was such a mustache as was once pasted on the face of Mack Swain, who played the villain in Keystone Comedies with Charlie Chaplin; it was vaster by far than the grease-paint whimsy of Groucho Marx—and it was real. Into the right eye-socket of the man now towering above you was screwed a dark blue monocle, a caricature of an eyeglass in a caricature of a face. As he held out his hand, the flesh around his left eye creased into many wrinkles and the whole face seemed to smile. You would know that he was holding back some of the strength of his grip.

If you met Woop outside his farmhouse in Normandy, near a curve of the lower Seine, he would almost certainly be followed by a large sorrel pony. He would drop an arm over his companion's neck and introduce her gravely. "This is Clementine. Clemmy's in love with me. She thinks I'm a horse."

But if you knew Woop a little better—as well as I knew him when I went to ask him to tell me about himself—you would understand that his self-mockery masked an acute sensitiveness about his appearance, as the mustache hid a feature that had been beaten out of recognition as a mouth. The eye behind the blue glass had been blinded by a Gestapo iron; his thinning brown hair was brushed back over a head from which large pieces of shattered skull had been removed; the face that had seemed to smile had been battered until it was incapable of smiling. That powerful body had been broken by some of the most accomplished sadists of Europe, had been wounded, as he had mentioned casually one day, twenty-seven times, and might now give out on him at any time. "I love life," he had said to me once. "I love it and I will not die." I wanted to know why he had sold the thing he loved—sold it dearly, little by little, a broken bone, a smashed cartilage, a burned eye at a time—until he had only a small amount of it left.

Woop is not only a cartoonist, although it is for his anti-Nazi drawings that he became known. By talent he is a painter, who paints, as another artist put it, "like a pupil of Vermeer's." By nature Woop is a militant idealist, and as such he had come to contain in his person much of the tragedy of Europe, or at least of that humanitarian Europe which once put hope in Marxism and now feels betrayed and lost.

I thought Americans would be interested to know why the son of a comparatively wealthy man became not an orthodox Communist but a practicing revolutionary who worked for Communism; how a sensitive artist could live as a workman, fight in several wars, and willingly submit to jail and torture out of belief that he was helping his fellow-man; and how, finally disillusioned, he could still think of his old comrades without bitterness and deny himself what he most wanted in life to help them—Woop, who would like to paint all the time, gives away money so fast that he is always in debt and must work hard to earn what he gives away. I thought that this was a kind of European that Americans ought to know about, since such men now look to America.

He told me his story—or as much of it as he could bring himself to tell—in a grove above the farmhouse, where there were wicker chairs and a table. I glanced across the table at his big, comic face, and reflected that it was a mark of arrogance. He could have left the sightless eye and the shapeless lips exposed. But then he would have been pitiful, and he would rather be laughed at than pitied. And so he was arrogant. He had a right to be, as he had a right to call himself, not William Wolpe, as he had been born in what is now Czechoslovakia, or Willie Wooping, as he had been known at school in England, but Woop—plain Woop.

"I look back at the wonderful, wonderful friends I had," said Woop. "There are too few left. They believed in something like liberty and justice and bringing up our children in peace—in something very normal. They got killed and they will never come back, and I am accusing everyone who has made it that they died for nothing. I profoundly believed against the fascists. Nazism is a construction of mind, not a political opinion. Nazis or Communists, short trousers or long trousers; it's only an optical illusion. Only someone who was tortured knows. Only someone who has been in prison knows what freedom is.

"I never really was a Communist," he went on. "I fought the things they fought. I thought there must be an economic

136

solution somewhere. I thought the Marxist solution was not a bad one. I thought you must have a guarantee of two or three generations properly brought up. Then people would learn to be decent. I thought the Russians would produce something, but I just watched the development of the Russian uniform and I knew. Now the Russians are like what I'm against. This century is killing individuals, and I don't like the Communists any more because they are contributing to that.

"I can't look at my life properly because I see horrible things. I was in a group of exactly 100 revolutionaries. Most of them are dead. We worked in the open. It was a simple fight, really. It was a fight for pennies for the workers. But it was a violent life. I was six feet three and strong, and they expected me to do things that I would just rather not do. I hate killing. I hate doing anything heroic. But sometimes I just had to do it. My fight with the Nazis goes back a long time. Back to 1920. They caught me in 1933. I was completely in their hands for two and a half years. I was doing anti-Hitler cartoons for the German press in those days, and to get hold of me was the most logical thing. I was told that I was Number 3 or 4 in the first Brown Book. I suppose I should have escaped. I didn't because I didn't honestly think I should. If I did the cartoons and the other things, I just had to be an example. I think my action was appreciated, by peasants and simple people. Besides, I thought life could not matter so much. I didn't quite realize what an experience I was in for.

Any story about concentration camps is still unbelievable. I can't talk about what they did to me.

"Once on a bridge in Budapest I ran into one of the Nazis who had tortured me. I didn't feel hate or anything, but I ran after him; I just couldn't let him go by. I said: 'Where are you now?' He said: 'I'm not a Nazi any more; you convinced me.' And I said: 'It is just too late,' and I threw him over the bridge. I hope he could swim."

Then he did talk a little about what they had done to him —breathing heavily, getting up once to walk around the table, then throwing himself back into the wicker chair. "They made me afraid for the first time in my life. I was afraid of sadism. I didn't know how to handle it. There is no sense in it when they sew buttons on your naked body. Or leave you for thirty-six hours in a cell not much wider than yourself, with electrified walls, so that if you sway and touch one it's all over. They kicked in my jaw and put out both eyes with hot steel rods. I was totally blind for almost a year, until in their crazy way they treated one eye and I got the sight of it back. There is no sense in it. You will not talk, and after a while they know it. So why not stop it or kill you? I didn't give anyone away. I think they just wanted to break me. A slave walks like a slave and a free man walks like a free man, and they hated it. Some of the guards cried when they brought me back to my cell. I did not hate them for their cruelty to me. Only when I was blind and couldn't paint. Once they broke both my wrists. I learned to draw with my toes. I hate them for that because I loved painting so much. You cannot break the fingers of a musician, even if he is your political enemy. It hurts me very much to have my face destroyed. I am an artist, and I loved my face.

"My mother killed herself because she didn't want to be afraid any more. It was while I was in prison in Prague. She wrote me a beautiful farewell letter, saying that someone should go to God and tell him what they were doing to me. She thought God would listen to her, even after she had committed suicide. She was an Irish Catholic, but she asked to be buried in a Jewish cemetery. She wanted to be with people who had suffered."

Woop leaned back and let out a deep breath, and I could see his body begin to relax. He looked at me and wrinkled his face into that impossible smile. "What is so wrong in the world is that people are afraid of facing facts—big facts. Partly they are afraid and partly they can't take it in. It makes them rather nice. It makes them childish, but it makes them rather nice. I don't believe in the next war. One bomb, and all the people die. There will be injustice, but we cannot afford another war. I don't mind people acting like children, but sometime someone must grow up and say: 'We cannot afford it. We cannot lose these people.'

"I was very bitter after the last war, very bitter. You remember what you hoped for, and you see what they are doing with it. I made everybody responsible for all the people I loved who were dead. I am kinder now, but sometimes in bars I do have fights. People do make stupid remarks about my face. The face is broken. The heart is not broken, and it is difficult to live like that, even if one is intelligent. . . ."

He walked with me to my car.

"You are going back to America. Something very good could come out of America, if you do not let yourselves be afraid. With three generations of peace, the working people everywhere would make a little money, stop being afraid, and learn to live. They should study, understand art and music. That doesn't just come; it takes hard work. But then maybe they would know how to live. I'm not a dreamer, I'm a hoper," said Woop. "God bless you."

He turned away his caricatured face and started back toward the house, walking, clumsily, like a free man.

13

From the end of November through Christmas Day the hours fell for Wert and for me, and so in my memory, not into days and weeks, but into three clear divisions: those spent with pain, those spent with others present, and those alone together.

What was left of his life—and what he gained from it and what he left from it to others and to me—was bought and paid for by torment. He thought a great deal about Woop, who had paid much more dearly in this coin. This is one reason why I have included part of the article he had written in 1950 about Woop, whom he loved. He thought also about Buchenwald, which he had seen at the time of its liberation. It had stayed always vivid in his consciousness as the terrible proof that prolonged and sufficient suffering could destroy the humanity of even very good and very strong men. He thought of what Woop had said to him one day: "You must tell people whatever they do under torture they must not blame themselves. No one may blame them and they *must not* blame themselves. Tell them this from me."

Wert never for an instant compared his own agonies with the deliberate infliction without alleviation of the greatest possible pain by men on others. The cancer was an impersonal torturer, although it became for us personified as evil. We had doctor and drugs and the freedom to fight it all on our side. Yet time and again Wert only barely managed, by a final effort of will, to keep from breaking, which to him meant screaming. As long as he could keep from screaming, or even moaning, and thus letting loose in the house the sound of agony for his children to hear, he wanted now to live through Christmas. It would be a pity, he said, to get near and then to spoil the day of the year that meant so much to the young by dying.

The left side of the intestines closed off for a while, and this was about the worst cancer could do, as the medical men in New York had told us, thinking he would be spared that. When the *crises* came then he would sit on the edge of something so as to touch a surface with as little of his body as possible. His face would draw down into an unrecognizable mask and he would whisper his instructions, afraid even of the use of his voice, telling me what drugs to hand him, what hypodermics to bring so that he, with cautious haste, could inject himself.

The medical side of this is beyond me. There is always enough of some anesthetic to kill any pain. There is also a period between onslaught and alleviation. If a man goes on living, there is a price on anesthetics, too, in disintegration. Wert insisted now upon making and maintaining his own decisions. Sometimes we called Cartier to come, more often we did not. I would go to his office sometimes to get advice and prescriptions. Like Danielson, Cartier saw no virtue in suffering. He did all he could, including trial shots of a slow-down drug, but when these seemed to bring on *crises* he agreed with Wert over cutting them out. He went so far beyond French regulations on morphine derivatives that the druggist telephoned him twice to ask if he knew what he was risking. He also believed truly and profoundly that it was his duty, at any price, to prolong life as long as he could. We almost always exceeded his dosages, not telling him until afterwards. What he prescribed was almost always short of being effective. We did not tell him the extent of our American supply, especially as other substitutes he tried, as well as a French form of liquid morphine, seemed to work better. I did not tell him of supplies of these from Paris and Bordeaux. I can't say whether we might have done better. Wert weighed with care the balance among pain, drugs, and bad reactions to drugs.

At one point when the left side was closed off, Cartier urged an operation. It was the "bag" operation and Cartier felt it would make the *crises* less frequent and fierce, at least for a while, by freeing the bowels and dispensing with gas. I retailed his lecture carefully to Wert.

"No doctor seems to count in what recovery from an operation is like, even a biopsy," Wert said grimly. "I'd be in a hospital, a bedridden body yelling for sedatives they could give or withhold, separated from you. I might be a little better afterwards, and I suppose I'd get used to what seems disgusting to think about now, but so what? To hell with it."

Cartier and I had a fight when I told him Wert refused, telling him deliberately in front of Wert so that he would not argue. Wert was sitting on the sofa, just pulled out of a *crise,* with his eyes closed. Cartier stood over me and I stood, arms akimbo, fishwife-style, at the end of the sofa. Cartier knew as well as I did that Wert could not follow rapid French when he was in such a weary state. Instead of accepting his decision with a shrug and a grimace, Cartier, moved beyond his professional concern, lit into me freely.

"You cannot let him refuse!" he said. "*You're* responsible. You're the well one. You and I should take him by force if necessary in an ambulance to the hospital. You cannot leave it to him. He is too sick. He is . . . This is the right thing to do!"

"If he wants it, we'll do it," I said, raising my voice as Cartier had raised his, tried almost beyond my own endurance. "It's his body, his life, his mind! His pain. He's not nuts or weak-minded. He is a man. He can do as he pleases to do."

"But he cannot go on like this," said Cartier. "It's your responsibility to make him . . ."

"Will the operation make him live?"

"No. No. But longer . . ."

"Then I won't argue with him. I have told him all you said, but I will not even argue with him, you hear?"

"I don't understand you. I don't understand either of you. It will make it better for a while."

"After it is worse, it will be better for a while. And then?"

"Then . . . then. . . ."

"When he wants to die, he can do that, too," I said.

"You can't let him kill himself!" said Cartier. "You cannot."

"Why not?"

"You would not kill him?"

"No! And I don't want him to die one day sooner, God knows, but do you understand me, it's up to *him* what he does!"

"You would help him do that!" he said in horrified comprehension. "I believe you would. This is serious. *You must not.*"

I might have said a dangerous thing, then, but Wert interrupted very quietly, with such an air of authority that we both obeyed him.

"Stop fussing," he said.

At the front door, out of Wert's hearing, Cartier said to me: "I do not understand this. But I must try to understand this. For he is the bravest of men. I tell you, Madame Wertenbaker, I never in my life expected to meet a man who might face his death this way. I never expected to meet such a man, *surtout* . . ." and he hesitated, I think about to say, "above all an American," but he said rather quaintly, *"surtout dans St. Jean-de-Luz."*

The physical side of this had to be important, though I don't mean to dwell upon it. I had to learn a form of self-protection then, as much for Wert's sake as for mine. As the dreadful *crises* became frequent, Wert taught me, and I learned, to go away inside myself, sit there or sleep at night, not to try to *be* there with Wert during them. I could neither share nor ease his pain by sympathetic suffering. My sympathy only twisted me so that I could not emerge from sympathy in time to share the free time with him. To make of this December what it was, I must think only of doing as quickly and efficiently as possible anything I could or he asked me to do and for the rest think quickly and quietly and hard of other things when his face was drawn down and he was alone inside himself fighting pain. It was hardest when the attacks came suddenly and he would convulse for an instant, his face distorted like a gargoyle's screaming in stone, soundless. When his face began to be his own again and at last he could turn his head carefully, he would look over at me. He would smile at last tranquilly and I could smile tranquilly back and then we could share in tranquillity his freedom from pain. "You can't imagine what it means when I come out of it and find you like that!" he said. Then we could have the hours for which he bore the others.

He felt the choice was truly free now, so long as he was silent. He only saw the children when he wanted them with him, when he could be natural, whether gruff or gay.

The characteristic loss of weight caused by cancer stripped the flesh from his bones until there was none left except some grotesque swellings. We used extra cushions for him to sit on and lean against in the big, soft chair by the fireplace. In time the left side seemed to clear a passage, for the gas problem grew less, and Cartier gave up the idea of an operation. The liver took over. On December 22nd he had, and lost, his last meal and gave up trying to eat, often unable to retain even the tea he continued to drink in quantities. He went to bed every night, but sleeping medicines worked for a very limited time and I would wake to find him sitting on the edge of the bed, a pillow on the side table where he could rest his arms. Unless he needed me and called, he would order me to sleep, saying I was dopey when I was short of sleep, and no fun.

Most days he dressed, although it began to take him an hour and then two. I bathed him when he wanted me to, as he sat on a stool beside the *bidet* in the bathroom. Shaving became a problem and his wrist too weak to strop his Rolls razor. I did that for him, and held the mirror, and he managed fairly regularly, sitting on the edge of the bed. I brought a barber and a manicurist from St. Jean to the house one evening, but they were so moved by the appearance of this old customer and friend that he did not want them again. Besides, it tired him even more than our slow arrangements while he managed for himself. As he was nearly shaven-headed when the barber finished, his hair grew too long only by his own standards.

Every day he moved down the steep stairs, step by step, to the chair by the fire in the little living room. And at night he went up again, while I walked behind him in case he should fall. Cartier only came to the house when I called him, and as time went on he was truly startled on each visit to find that Wert could still negotiate the stairs. "Impossible. Impossible," he would mutter. But Wert did, tottering down them and up again, tottering like a free man.

His heart and his lungs continued strong and youthful-acting, although his pulse would often accelerate wildly and sometimes he took a shot of camphor. One day he said: "My God, it takes a hell of a lot to kill a man!"

14

The day came when I finally told Ama and Gashousha that Wert would never recover, was dying. They were grave and stricken, although they could scarcely have failed to guess. When I told them he knew this they were at first horrified and then awed. "We would never let anyone know," Ama said. "We would deny it." "The priest who comes says, 'No. No. I shall see you again tomorrow.' Never would one be told," said Gashousha, shaking her head. "The doctor and the priest do not even tell the person closest to anyone who is dying. Only someone not so close." "He knows!" they said to each other, over and over then, and still say now: "He knew!"

The news gradually rippled out, to a few people in the village and to a few more friends in the rest of the world.

The old Basque peasant who worked the old-fashioned farm lying beside the road between our house and the tower came to our back door and spoke to Ama, but would not come in. "Tell Monsieur," he said, his closed face and monumental bulk very still, "that he is a fine man who has said 'Bon jour' to me so gracefully for the years he has passed my house. Tell him I should be happy to do anything, at any hour of the day or the night, if it would help him. Tell him I look at the view of La Rhune from below the tower every day for him. I understand his bravery, although I have only said bon jour to him. He is too fine a man to die and I am sad!" Dominique Toyos came, his fishing-boat-captain's face stern. "When you need me," he said to me, "I will come. Do not ask for anyone else." Yet Dominique is an arrant coward about such things, and would not help to lay out an uncle of his because he said he was frightened of dead flesh.

I wrote to my sister Julie and told her, writing while they were clear and fresh certain things Wert felt about the children in case it should ever devolve on her as guardian to carry them out. I suggested she not tell our mother, whose profound concern would be for me, her firstborn. I did not need it now, having Wert's courage. I would need it later. Julie wrote back and said that perhaps only someone as deeply married as she was could understand that for us to have this time together, in full knowledge, was a blessing. "Dwight and I would want to know it and have it, if we could."

Wert's brother, Peyton, wrote and said: "We had such an insanely cheerful letter from sister Ningy who saw you in New York that we are worried." His wife added a postscript to me: "Please tell us how is old sweetie pie." Wert dictated a letter to me for them, humorous, flat, and factual. Peyton answered: "We'll come if you want us, not if you don't. There are worse things than dying."

By telephone, I told Stephen Laird, who lived in Paris with the warm, handsome woman he had married and their two children. It was Steve, younger than either of us, whose uncompromising decency had kept a tense emotional situation involving the three of us from becoming an ugly one, one that would have harmed us all as well as hurt us. Steve never confused his emotions and had kept his male friendship and working relationship with Wert, his admiration and affection, separate from the rest. His first question was whether Wert could kill himself if he wanted to. I said yes, and he said, "I'll do anything for Wert, you know," which I did.

Unable to lie to him, Suzie Gleaves had told Irwin Shaw in

London. Irwin telephoned across the Channel several times and finally, in mid-December, without admitting that he knew, said he was coming to Ciboure to spend a few hours with Wert. It was the day of an "awful crise" when he called and I told Irwin I could not say in advance whether Wert could see him or not. "I'll take a chance," he said. "If he's too sick, I'll talk to you and go away." On this basis, I was very glad he was coming.

There were others near enough to come who would have come, but we hesitated over the strains and the risks involved. The hours were too precarious, and it required a certain relaxed toughness to come upon Wert suddenly now, to see him and this piece of time whole, without an overbalancing emotion of distress.

We wanted Nathalie Kotchoubey, who had been Wert's "office daughter" in Paris, if only to see her blush again. Wert had hired her as a bilingual typist and quickly discovered her talents, demanding that she become a reporter, and never mind her blushes and her shyness. Successful and poised as she had grown, she always blushed still near Wert because she had been so shy a darling.

One early December day when Wert was especially well, we considered asking Orson Welles down for an afternoon, to recite Shakespeare and to talk Bible, bulls, and Botticelli with Wert in the little living room, as he had done several times in the summer after they had met in Pamplona. He was at his brilliant best around Wert, and delighted in it, as did Wert.

The Kaufmans telephoned, not wanting to leave Paris for Connecticut without seeing us again, but we were afraid of a visit. "They will be quiet and lovely," said Wert, "but it will make them too sad. It was such a perfect summer."

We sent a message to our old friend Janet Flanner, who rarely left her tiny hotel room with the grand view of Paris for anything that did not contribute to her *New Yorker* letters, wanting and expecting no reply. She wrote me late in January, with the special perspective she has on any scene or situation, political, personal, or national. Her reaction to the little she knew of what had happened to us was the first thing that took me beyond sharing private grief to think that the book Wert had believed should be written out of such an experience and which only I was left to write must still perhaps one day be written. Beginning "Dearest Lael," she went on rapidly from expressing her sense of loss and recall to say:

I want to tell you how wonderful I think it was that you consciously shared what was inevitable between you & practiced truth not illusion during those final months. It changed everything but the fact itself, alas, & excited my appreciation & imagination by its courage & its vital grave common-sense, so that as long as he could live he was living on truth & knew, as was suitable to & characteristic of him, exactly what was transpiring. You made a new kind of acceptance of death in terms of still being alive, of consciousness, of conscience, of reality; it was a new kind of drama of domesticity, in the highest terms that drama can be used, as conflict with an ending, dependent upon characters in movement; I was really seized by the importance of this contribution you both made, as an example, as an admirable and extraordinary choice, unique so far as I know, & I wrote it down as a private event of hitherto unknown philosophy in my diary.

It had seemed to both Wert and me that his choice of knowing was natural, not admirable, merely consistent with the kind of man he was and with the rest of his life. It literally did not occur to me that perhaps I should not tell him the truth, whatever the truth was, until Jim's opposition to it in New York. I admit, with no pride in it, to a simple and uncomplex mind, which I have often regretted because when Wert was at his subtlest and most profound I was by no means his intellectual equal. When he extracted the promise that I would keep nothing from him, it was for fear I would be qualmish or careless over details, or might weaken if offered a choice of his living as a cripple. The surprise of others at his attitude surprised us. The choice of not knowing is a free choice, too, but I cannot believe the choice we made is either "new" or "rare."

I only hope someone respects me as I respected him when my time comes. Such a definitive medical situation is, of course, rare enough. When it occurs, I know there are certain doctors who will define it, given the readiness of the patient to understand, and leave with such a one pills he "must not take" so many of, defining thus a fatal dose. I know of one young man who called a friend, in such circumstances, and told him to come over on Tuesday. "No, not Thursday," he replied cheerfully to the suggestion. "That's too late. I'll be dead." But even in much less certain circumstances, to know the truth or even the fallible if honest opinions of others seems to me the privilege of the man or the woman and not something to be decided by society (which is not harmed by the death of a private citizen) or by a code designed for all people without respect to individual choice. When someone does not want to know, he will not know if he can help it, and should not have to know. I make no argument for "euthanasia" imposed by the judgment of men on others. I am not arguing the right of a man to foreshorten his days, either. I am demanding that knowledge and truth should never be withheld by its possessor from any man capable of understanding them and wishing rightfully to have them. There was a splendid old man, the father of a friend, who had survived by sheer will three nearly fatal periods in a year of illness. He was given up for lost, but not told, only guessing how near he came. He said to me a few months ago: "Did you tell your husband the truth and all of it all the time?" "Yes," I said. "I want to shake your hand," he said.

We did not tell the children, although we did not lie to them. Chris discovered that it was cancer, when he asked, and with considerable alarm unearthed all the statistics he could find. Wert told him it was, indeed, quite possible to die of it, and to take it straight if he did. Timberlake went visiting for a few days and when she returned she noticed, for the first time, how ravaged Pop was. "Only your eyebrows are just the same," she said mournfully, smoothing them with her fingers.

Wert's relationships with other people he liked, including his children, were both warm and reserved. His own emotional intimacy was with his wife. Having no easy sympathy either for himself or for anyone else when a state of anxiety could be resolved by a small amount of good sense or good will, he did not readily offer or receive minor confidences. Liking rarely affected his judgment, and I considered his judgment excellent, but then we nearly always agreed about people. He did not give a damn whether anyone liked him or did not. That was up to them. He did not care whether people he liked liked other people he liked or did not. He was broadly tolerant, with a few intolerances of depth and power which provided him with a vigorous hatred of certain individuals and made for him a few vital enemies. Equable in most disagreements, he enjoyed argument or discussion of differences of opinion, but was quickly bored with a repetition of fixed opinions. Having once stated his own and examined his opponent's for anything which might modify his own, he would resort, in such cases, to antic and fanciful responses for his private amusement. I remember John Osborne, who succeeded him as foreign editor of *Time,* and for whom he felt great affection which survived many important disagreements. Consumption of bourbon whiskey increased John's standpat argumentativeness and decreased what there was of Wert's. Late in an evening, "You *can't* mean that," John would say, yanking his forelock and peering outraged into Wert's straight face.

Wert disliked dependent or unequal relationships of any kind. More than one young man and woman had offered him the father relationship, especially during the time when many worked under him and were provided by him as their boss with the maximum protection he could manage for everything from raises in salary through their opinions and self-respect. It was appealing, he said, flattering, touching—and a trap, dangerous, for it was not a proper relationship between grown people of any age.

To me it was a matter of grave joy when two moral and self-disciplined men met and spoke together, often very little alike and trying to convince each other of nothing. Such men have in common that they rarely make either leaders or followers of others and that neither failure nor success has more than a superficial effect on them. I remember Wert, for all his six foot one, looking slight and fragile beside Woop when Woop said: "I'm not a dreamer, I'm a hoper." Beside the small, pudgy body of Pablo Casals, he looked enormous, spare, and powerful. "I am not talking politics, I am talking morals," said Casals to Wert. With John Hersey, he looked older and John looked younger than the actual difference in their years, but the effect was of the total unimportance of this. When he and Jean Valdeyron were gleefully translating the Jabberwocky into French and back again or discussing politics or philosophy, the national differences between an attractive American and an attractive Frenchman were both emphatic and unimportant. My impressions, those times, were of the wonder of human communication, not of words, of the momentary enlargement of the world that contained such men standing thus upright together.

It took a lot of years for me to see him justly with other women. Women were attracted by him and vice versa. If he disciplined his actions, as he did, he did not deny or evade his reactions, which were naturally sexual, and he was also a flirt. I was gracious enough about those girls and women whose flesh was their chief charm. Indeed, I find it alarming when any man does not pinch, or wish to, certain bottoms. Intelligent women in their middle years who were also physically charming made me stiffen as to a threat. Yet they were only a threat if, through jealousy, I tried to discipline his relations with them instead of letting him do this himself. In the last years I had grown, in love, in intelligence, in discipline, and enjoying myself the company of such women as much as that of men, accepted the peripheral addition of an attraction between the sexes.

So other people added unto us and took nothing away. There was very little time for other people now, for anything added. When Jean and Nicole Valdeyron, our nearest French friends, came from Paris to St. Jean-de-Luz for their Christmas vacation, I went alone to see them. I told them the truth and that Wert did not want to see them.

"He would like you to remember your American friend as he was," I told them, using the formal *"vous,"* although our valued and carefully nurtured friendship had become very close over the years. It was based on respect for each other's privacy and national differences as well as mutual appreciation of many things and of each other's languages, which none of us handled as well as we should have liked to do. "His physical appearance distresses his vanity and he is too weary to speak French." Delicate-minded, sensitive, and devoted to each other, they understood everything exactly, even how he could see Irwin, with whom he had been in wartime and who spoke with easy American usage his own language, and not wish to see Jean. "He sends you his dear love," I said. "And we are here for you if there is anything we can do to help him, to help him die when he wishes to die," they said. "We love him and we love you."

Jean telephoned a specialist in Paris who had had a most extraordinary record of cancer cures, confirming for himself that nothing could be done in Wert's case. At midnight one night, when I had called to ask them, they came to the house bringing a box of vials of the form of morphine that seemed the most effective, which they had hijacked out of a surgeon they knew with a hospital in Bordeaux.

Irwin's choice of a day was fortunate. Wert wrote in his *carnet:* "Puny but good. Shaw here. Biriatou."

We spent five hours over lunch at Biriatou, sitting on the terrace of that small Basque restaurant in that tiny and perfect little village. The sun shone with the brilliance that only stormy weather on a rainy coast can produce as an aftermath. The two men, the one from Brooklyn and the one from Charlottesville, rejoiced in the Basque country they both loved deeply as an expansion of their love of many places.

We were alone on the terrace. We were very gay. Irwin's immense laughter made the vine leaves overhead tremble. Wert's laughter was a harmonizing undertone and mine was part of the trio.

Man and wife, Wert and I said to each other certain things I have repeated as spoken. Such subjects of conversation between rational grown people as morals, politics, literature, reduced and summarized, sound too often like senatorial or professorial baby-talk. Reminiscences, obliquely approached and lightly handled in speech, turn into written narrative, and how Wert detested narrative conversation anyway, refusing to label an exchange of "stories" as conversation at all. Any odd topic or narrative may serve wit—and Irwin has a gift of narrative wit, as Wert had of decorative and commentarial wit, to which my (as Eric Linklater remarked of a character in a novel) "principle contribution to humor was good humor." Given the space and freedom of a novel, a few writers can project in synthesized dialogue the interplay of grown minds already familiar with each other. Of these hours I can give you only the end.

"It was great, just great," said Irwin, embracing Wert by the shoulders, Spanish-style, to leave.

As I drove Irwin down from the house to the train he cried, steadily and unashamed, the way soldiers do in war sometimes, I think, over courage, not over death.

Wert read a book that week, a new one I had brought back from the United States. Except for Montaigne and for glancing at a few favorites, he had not been reading, preferring to talk, think, or listen to Bach. He picked it up one day after I had read him a sentence that delighted me. It was *The Flint Anchor,* by Sylvia Townsend Warner, which told a quiet period story and ended with the death of an old man. "I can't die until I finish it," he said. "It would be rude to a perfect artist. What prose. Tranquillity over depth." This is a tribute he paid to a contemporary writer. Another tribute was his sense of the living presence in the house of Alexander and Gina Brook, whom he loved. Alex's portrait of me hung in the living room and the artist was there, in his painting.

Stephen Laird came down on December 22nd, bringing Christmas packages for our children and a tear-stained note from his wife and some barbiturate suppositories of a strength I had been unable to obtain. He said to Wert, as they sat alone by the fire, "You are the best I've known in my life. Tell me what you want me to be or do."

Steve told me this when I took him to the train, and I asked Wert what he had answered. "I told him never to lie to himself or anybody else and that he was a good man, Steve, because he is." Wert wrote Jacqueline Laird a note, although it cost him so much pain to write anything that he had stopped trying any more on the 19th. "Cherish your man," he wrote to her. Coming from him it was tribute, not admonition, for he was fatherly to no one except his own children.

Wert tried to eat while Steve was there. We even went out to lunch, in Ascain, for he could not go farther in the car any more, however barefooted I drove. That was the end of leaving the house, as well as of eating. The notes on his drugs became very long: 8:30, 9:05, 9:45, 10:40, 11:05, 12, 12:40, 1:20 and so on. Most nights were sleepless.

Chris and Timberlake prepared our Christmas, as they had done since Chris was seven. This year Chris found and cut a tree in the pine woods near us and he and Timberlake decorated it with that combination of taste and total lack of it natural to most enthusiastic youngsters. It was in the dining room this year. There was a French *crèche* on the sideboard and stars strung from tinsel over the dining table. Christmas Eve by the fireplace they hung stockings, the roomiest they could find, this time a hideous pair of rubberized winter hose commandeered from Ama. The children looked seasonally flushed, anticipatory, joyful.

"You're right attractive when you're good," Wert told them. "Now go to bed before you spoil it." As I sat stuffing the stockings, Wert reflected, "I don't find myself taking last looks, at them or the countryside or anything."

By long-established family tradition, the stockings were transferred during their sleep to the ends of their beds. Besides fruit, candy, and nuts, a small package present and a few toy-trinkets were included. They were to stay in bed, eating and playing, until their parents chose to rise, breakfast, dress, and declare that it was Christmas-tree time, an arrangement among others of ours designed to keep the generations from mingling in a manner that precluded Wert's enjoyment of his offspring and hence theirs of him.

So illness was not underlined and it was quiet in the house when he was able to sleep a little while on Christmas morning. At ten he went downstairs in his dressing gown, so weak that to dress would have meant another two hours for them to wait. Their patient impatience exploded and they burst from their beds and tumbled down after him. He unobtrusively disappeared into the living room for most of the tree and package revels, and for the visit of Ama's five grandchildren and the Toyos boys. Afterwards he came slowly into the dining room and sat on a chair there to be shown the loot, to accept his own, and to give each of us a special symbol of his continuing love. To Chris he presented his own gold wristwatch, the one he had worn since before Chris was born. To Timberlake, the thin, chaste watch chain that had been his father's and for which we had bought a matching locket for her to wear around her child's stalk-like neck on the chain. Ama and Gashousha had come in to watch, but both of them turned away and went out the back door and into the garage. Chris's and Timberlake's thanks were awed and gentle.

That night Timberlake said, "Oh, I'm so happy, Pop!" and Chris said with a great sigh, "This has been the best day of my whole life."

15

"Oh, the intensity of the beginning and the intensity of the end!" exclaimed Wert.

It is this phrase that I hear in his voice when I think about that part of our December, the part spent alone with neither pain nor any person with us.

I remember his head as he spoke and the look of it, and his eyes and the look in them, and his hands as he stretched his fingers, and what he said afterwards and what I said.

We had been picking over our memories that hour, as if they were spread around us, taking our leisure to handle and turn and lift them to the light. Going back to our first meeting, we had realized how much our commitment to like each other had preceded that meeting. Long before I met him I had worked for him and become dependent on him as my editor for his judgment, his delicate, powerful liberalism, and his belief that truth was the only servant of good in journalism. He had, he told me, sometimes found my analyses politically ingenuous, my preconceptions artless and uncritical, although mercifully unsystematic, but he had known from reading my cables that what I sent was as truthful as I could make it, and that what I said I had seen, or quoted as having heard, had been seen and heard. It was a very political period, then, and easy for reporters or editors to lose sight of truth in conviction.

When we met in England, Wert had the freedom of his

divorced bachelorhood, during which he had been by no means alone. I had the freedom of my husband's youthful belief that freedom of the individual extended also and broadly to the partnership of marriage. We had no intention, either Wert or I, of taking advantage of this. Wert had very nearly made up his mind to marry a beautiful woman who shared many of his tastes, especially in music and art, and he did not want to change the image in his dream of making, at last, a till-death good marriage. I believed my marriage, which had many strong and happy values, would improve with age and a more adult conception of the disciplines anything so important required. The head of the London office, seeing that Wert enjoyed my company, assigned to me without guile the duty of assisting him to see England. We were not struck by love. It just came about.

There were the three schoolgirls I knew in Dover, where I took him. They clustered around me and giggled and said, "Wot did 'e s'y, Lael?" every time Wert muttered happily at them in his Virginia-accented American, twice-muffled by the depth of his voice. We really looked at each other with love rather than only sympathy first over their black, blond and red heads. Wert had a cold in Liverpool and I washed his handkerchiefs and "ironed" them on the surface of a claw-footed tub in the hotel bathroom, a system his mother had employed. We connived together to escape the sightseeing program an over-eager-beaver from the Ministry of Information wanted us to fill, and went, instead, to see the things we wanted to see, which were the same things. "You dance so badly," I said to him one night, surprised that he did anything badly, and he walked off the floor, leaving me deserted and conspicuous. When I rejoined him, regretting my natural candor, he said happily, "The excuse I've been looking for all my life. I'll never have to dance again." On the grass at Oxford, he said solemnly, "I am a very lucky man." In High Wickham, I cried out, "Why, you're an affectionate man, *too,*" knowing, too, that it was affection and not love or admiration

I could not live without as daily bread. And all the time there was the easy, relaxed pleasure of our talking, about anything, everything.

So the intensity of love grew quietly and gaily between us, in spite of our reluctance, gathering us into marriage. Our beginning climaxed and culminated in the birth of our first-born, my very firstborn, a birth that was hilarious, uncomplicated, and intense with overwhelming tenderness.

"The intensity of the beginning," repeated Wert as we talked about it— "And the happiness in between," he went on.

His body was all but gone and his head was a skull, with the fine, sweet skin drawn tight over bones. All the lesser qualities, good, bad, and petty, had been drawn out of his face.

Staring at him, I said, "I've teased you since the first about not really being handsome, and I still don't think you really were. But you are now. I've never seen anything as beautiful as your head right now."

"Ah," he said, "you know how to make a man feel good."

With a twist of guilt in my heart, I brought up the time I had betrayed him and us by my behavior, and he had betrayed us, too, by his irrational violence toward me, when it had seemed for a year afterwards that we should have to settle for so much less than the intense hopes and quiet promises of our beginning.

He made a gesture as if to take that old guilt in his hands and break it over his knee. He wiped out all guilt, including my nagging sense that I had made him, an orderly perfectionist, a most sloppy and clumsy wife. "Yes, you've clumsy hands," he said, "and all that. But do you know, now, watching how you try not to be messy, I find your messiness —endearing. And do you know that taking care of me, doing these things you've had to do, you've never hurt me? For all your awkwardness, you've never hurt me." He had time and perception, outside of any framework of confession, punishment, and absolution, to leave me free of guilt or regret toward him, for anything done or undone: to leave me grief without guilt.

It is this I should like to say, offering it with humility as wisdom, to everyone who loses someone he has loved and, inevitably, done less well by than he would like to have done: The dead don't, can't, want guilt or regret. . . . How fancy and absurd to speak thus of the dead.

It was Wert who insisted that I must continue to write other than as a reporter. Having married my editor, I tried to keep him at editing me, but he would never correct or change anything of my own I wrote—except to punctuate it, for he was a precisionist and I merely floured my prose with commas and colons. My faults or virtues were mine and he refused to tamper except to talk about the work. But when a paragraph was too fancy, murky, turgid or absurd, he would put a small cross in the margin. When I theorized, a question mark. When I produced a cliché with an air of discovery, he would write in the margin: "Now, Lael!" Now I am without his marginal safeguards, for it is since my editor died that I have learned and want to say how clean is grief without guilt.

He understood how this grief would be, and that it must be guiltless. He knew that the worst of it would be that I could not tell him about it, except into the past, from which he could no longer make his always fresh and unpredictable comments, from which he could give me no new comforting.

How much I have wanted to tell him since he died, in the intensity of his absence.

Someone asked me, diffidently, last summer if I should not like to try to get in touch with Wert. She knew a medium, and a friend of hers had "reached" and been comforted by her dead father. "Hell, no," I said, unprepared for the suggestion and therefore impolite. "Wert didn't even like to be called to the telephone when he was alive. If he hasn't changed and is somewhere else, he certainly doesn't want to be called to a *medium*. Besides, although he didn't think he'd be, if I thought he was 'out there,' in a state of waiting for me and wanting me, do you think I'd hang around here to die? I'd settle the children with my sister and go!" I am sure Wert would have laughed, at me, at the woman's alarmed expression, and told me not to talk so foolishly. Anyway, even such casual demi-speculation amused him no more than the "if's" and "if only's" of daydreams. The earth was enough, life as it was and you dealt with it was enough, and a good man was worth trying to be for the sake of being one.

I should like to have quoted him the lines in Lil Hellman's adaptation of Anouilh's *The Lark*. When I heard them, I cried them again silently, as if to him.

The Promoter says to Joan of Arc, "Do you believe that man is the greatest miracle of God?" and Joan says, "Yes," and then her great heresy, "What I am I will not denounce. What I have done I will not deny."

When the Michelin Guide came out, in the spring of 1955, I wanted to race with it to Wert, to tell him his *New Yorker* article, "The Testing of M. Thuillier," for which our research had been so joyous, had a happy ending. M. Thuillier kept his third star.

Most of all I wanted to tell him about the first months when I stayed alone except for the village and the children. We were not sure what this would be like, although Wert was right to suggest that I stay if I could, tough as it would be, and it was tougher than I thought it would be.

He would have had a fey "Wertenbaker medical theory" about why my winter-white skin turned quite black the night he died and stayed dark for two days. He would have understood and approved the queer elations of absolute grief, my abstract joy in the quality of his death, the quick, easy laughter when something small and funny happened in the midst of desolation, how the view of the mountains continued so beautiful and no reproach.

There was even comedy, although not for me at the time, in acrimonious battle done with the undertaker to get the kind of coffin he'd demanded for himself, wanting simple pine. The undertaker managed to imply, hiding behind the pocket handkerchief of his mournful air, that I was a stingy virago and obviously had not cared a sou for the dear departed.

Friends and family rallied so close from whatever distance, although I made them stay physically away. The feeling within his old corporation, in spite of everything, was that they had twice lost the best of men. The four Basque fishermen who carried his coffin yanked their berets over their faces and swore in Basque and cried tears. Timberlake saw a half-empty whiskey bottle out on the sideboard some weeks afterwards and said, "Oh, Pop!" in the most touching tone and burst into tears. I would like him to know how the terrible sorrow of his children turned to pride and the ease with which they spoke and speak of him, never mixing their tenses.

And I would like to quote him Chris's epitaph, so exactly the one to suit Wert. The day after he died, in the afternoon, Chris, deeply shaken, bereft, who had spoken little, brightened suddenly and said: "You know, Pop was lucky. He learned to play *Sol y Sombra* before he died."

We had planned our old age sometimes, in the past, discounting Wert's intuitive conviction that he was unlikely to survive the statistical average in his immediate family, which lay in the middle sixties. We would grow into each other with age like gnarled old trees, we thought, and would settle our roots in some tranquil place. If we were indigent, he would return to copyreading, which he loved, and blink beneath a green eyeshade, an old man writing expert heads for the front page of an old newspaper in a new day. If we had an income, we would find sun and a wide porch to drink and rock upon.

Claiming that if he ever lost his happy, high-handed pride in his maleness and its rights, his crotchets would become insupportable, I made him promise, in a bar in Pamplona, that he would run in the *encierro,* running through the dawn streets in front of the day's fighting bulls, in July the year he was seventy. This, I argued, would either restore his proper pride in spite of his years, or would provide him with a glorious male end on the horns of a bull.

"I fooled you," said Wert now. He did not mention again the other plans we had made for the years we would not have. "I won't have to run."

During this time, this month of December, I don't believe we were separated except by pain or sleep, not even by disparate thoughts, for more than an hour in a day. I no longer went to the doctor's office, it took too long, but telephoned for prescriptions. When he could eat no longer, I ran into the kitchen and ate with the children, with their casual haste, in minutes. With children's usual understanding of genuine emergency, they did not ask for any more of either of us than they were given. I was grateful for being where there were no necessary distractions. Even a few minutes' separation made us both restless. We might miss some ineffable moment of communication.

Occasionally I had to do an errand in St. Jean-de-Luz. I would try to contain my haste as I wheeled the car back up our hill, which had two sharp, slithery curves. Once, coming back, I became so frantically aware of the emptiness of the front seat, without Wert, that I could not stop weeping when I walked in the house. "I'll be so lonely," I cried out to Wert. "I'm afraid."

"Yes," he said somberly. "I know. Just don't panic. Keep on with our gamble as long as you can, but do anything you have to, love. Go back home and go to work when you need to. But I think, if it doesn't hurt you too much and you don't need comfort or distraction too badly, if you can—though I don't think I could—you should stay here for a year. Then nothing you ever do after is likely to be the wrong thing for you. And nothing you ever do or say or are afterwards can ever hurt the dignity of my memory."

He was not worried about leaving me the responsibility

for loving and raising Chris and Timberlake and letting them go. "You aren't possessive, but just don't get sacrificial," he said. "It isn't good for kids. You think not, but I hope you do find another man to love and make as happy as you've made me, and please know you have my unqualified blessing if you do." Then he laughed, a robust bass chuckle. "Hell, I'm not afraid of your settling for a second-rate man out of loneliness, Lael. Look at you. That's a formidable face. That jaw gets longer every year. You're a right formidable dame after so many years being *my* woman. You'd scare hell out of a second-rate man."

"Stick to Bach, Mozart and the early Italians for a year," he advised me. We had been playing the Second Brandenburg Concerto on the battered record player, which seemed about to, and did indeed, die with the master it had served for fifteen years. "You'd better wait for Beethoven, and if you find yourself listening to Schubert too soon, don't."

He was right about music, but after a year, when I could handle the emotions released by music, I found the Verdi Requiem the best for certain commemorative nights, celebrating as it does the loss of a man, not the transposition of a soul. I remember Wert listening to it in our first New York apartment, lying in the bathtub on Sunday mornings, a glass of orange juice and his cigarettes beside the tub, the doors open through the hall so that the crescendos could resound and the pianissimos be heard, loving it.

"Everything I have, everything I've loved, is yours, with all my love," he said.

I tried to thank him, overwhelmed and stretched with gratitude for all he had given me. For growth and children and love and music and wine and food and France and Spain —and most of all for himself and for his severe demands on me, for his demands which all added up to one demand: that I be for him the very best that I was, not different, but the best. This is a very difficult and irksome and often impossible thing to be. But it is the finest of all demands.

"Thank you for taking everything I had to give," said Wert. "Everything. That's rare."

He did not have time to write much more than I have included here of *Sixty Days in a Lifetime*. One early note for it reads: "Singular feeling that neither of the middle decades belonged to me, that at some point I went into false personality, & recovered true one only when I was 40. (A way of excusing sins and follies incident to discovery and growth?) My childhood & my middle age now seem to have been my life—at least the life I can remember with pleasure and the sense of having given. . . . & aren't 30 *good* years enough? I have 30 yrs. to relive & realize in maybe 90 days—every 3 days a year. (Do summary of Gib if not time for all.)" Then his estimate of the time he had was scaled down to sixty days, from which he drew his projected title.

Now there were obviously few days left, and those on which he could do "a little work" were still fewer. For the sake of his final serenity, and his conception of how to die well, he wanted to understand himself and his life as he left. For this, after that week of being a "patient," he was grateful that it was cancer which was killing him. It tortured him, but then it left him free between times. He was afraid that another disease, feverish, or treated by antibiotics, involving him wholly, or even leaving him comfortable and weak in bed, might have enslaved him as recurrent agony did not. He was no mystic who could move into the life of the spirit, as my father, a priest, might have done, for instance, separated from his manhood and his body. So there were compensations that it was cancer. "'A slave I do not have to be,'" he said, pointing out one line in Montaigne, "'except to Reason, and I can scarcely even manage that.'"

Having observed himself, as writers wish to do, with as much abstraction as he could muster through the years, he would have liked to sum himself up. It was not easy for him, even close as he was to his own complexities.

Going back to his childhood, to those first fifteen years, he knew that he had been neither warped nor blighted during them. This gave him a base which helped him to recover later, whole, from destructive periods in his life. His sense of honor, his headstrong pursuit of happiness and his ability to achieve it, his sense of identity with all mankind as a man, were rooted there. The first began as ancestral and Virginian. The second began with himself as a happy and headstrong little boy. The third began with his schooldays after his family moved to Newcastle, Delaware, where his comrades were the children of fiercely poor factory laborers whom he found tougher and gentler and better to be with than the boys known, by existing standards, as "his own kind."

There is a note left in the tower labeled "Theme for something" in which he wrote: "The capacity for happiness is the most valuable trait parents should nurture in their children. If a man is happy, he will give happiness to others. If happiness is taken away from him, he is still better off than if he had never had it." (There's an unconnected note on the bottom of the page: "Ambitious men have ambitious eyebrows.")

He found it hard later to return to Virginia, his first great love, and this grieved him. To him love, like loyalty, was not divisible. If you must reject one part, one loyalty, one friend, one country, for another, you must lose as well as gain. Loss for the sake of gain, as sin for the sake of righteousness, was no less loss and sin. He would have liked to return and settle there, freely and often. If they remembered him as a child, and he remembered them as children, and they and he allowed men to have grown from boys, those who had stayed and those who had gone away and returned, it was good. But they could only accept him if he was a man to whom nothing of importance had happened while he was away. He was not the boy he had been, to them, but the young man. He was the Wertenbaker whose mother was a Peyton . . . the one who had outdrunk his classmates at the

University, had written a book that older Virginians kept upstairs and still did not admit to having read . . . the one who had had three wives, been, done . . . but never the man who had thought about what he had been and done. "I could only come back if I embraced the legend," he wrote once, "and I could not bring myself to do that."

His years had paralleled those of the century and the changing decades had all influenced him, for he had never stopped growing in any one of them. Curious, critical, too vigorous, often combative, he had grown erratically, rebelliously, and contemporaneously.

Looking back on the twenties and thirties, as well as at the American heritage preceding their rebellions, he had made notes in the past year for *The Time of Enchantment,* which was to cover this twenty-year span.

He had old man Baron say to his son: "It's not simply a set of old-fashioned manners you people are casting aside. It's not only morals in the old-fashioned sense. That you show yourselves drunk in public and that you wallow with young girls in the back seats of cars, and with your friends' wives, isn't the important thing. The important thing is that you've cast aside a basic principle of the commercial civilization that produced you. Never mind the absolute value of that principle. It's enough that it has given men control over their weaknesses and their passions—even, a little, over their fate. —What you sign for you make good, your name on a marriage license or a note or a check. —Your cold checks, your installment buying, the man who accepts failure to pay his honorable debts. . . . Where's the honor? The man who cleaves to a stricken wife, who keeps his obligations, cost him what it will—you've seen us without happiness clinging to honor, and so you have chosen happiness, but for that you can't get credit: you have to pay for it in advance."

Of the thirties he had noted: "Something is to be done with their joy (in the 30s) in throwing off all morality. The 1920s got rid of sex-drinking scruples, but other standards of old times remained: can't lie, steal, cheat, etc. Now a new morality offered to make them free of those & they embraced the opportunity as joyously—and as thoughtlessly—as their seniors by ten years had embraced drinking and sex in bushes. (For them, drinking boring with end of prohibition —& sex boring as bores all after experimentation & before expertism.) Attraction of word 'decadence' in early 1920s. . . ."

Critical of them, Wert was not a man at odds with his times. It was the key to himself he lost for a time, losing control of his life thus, so that most of what happened to him was fortuitous. With stubborn impulsiveness and emotional violence, he got himself into situations which prevented the fulfillment he was seeking, in love, in work. When his personal equation was at its most destructive, he quit his job and tried to write for himself without any of the tranquillity necessary to him for writing. Later, caution and a sense of conventional obligation would not let him leave a new job and a sick wife to go as a reporter to the Spanish War, although his wife could support herself and he was soon to divorce her, at her wish, and the reporting job on the war was the work he wanted to do.

"I hurt people then," said Wert, talking of this time. "Never on purpose, but I did, and I hurt me. Now—since—I've hardly hurt anyone. I've hurt *you* because I beat on you, but that's all right. You're better for it. If I had died in 1938, I'd have died an utter failure, in love, in work, as a man. I've got the rest to be thankful for."

Recurrently in his life he had tried to establish the form of life which would give substance to his dream, a common enough one, of how to live most fully. Like another man's dream of a farm which will pay, or a small, successful business of his very own, or high adventure which he can finance by having it, it was simpler to dream than to manage. He wanted a family to love, to write as he pleased for his work and his living, and to enjoy himself thoroughly in many countries when he had earned it by working, not later, but simultaneously. His earlier attempts had failed, both financially and emotionally. Perhaps it was fear of failure that postponed this last try, for he had stayed on at Time, Inc., two years too long, he felt, in the period after the war. But then he committed himself to his dream and we set off.

You cannot recommend such a life to anyone else, even when you have managed it, even when you have found that this is indeed how to live. It is precarious, full of vexations and problems. You need luck, whatever else you have. Remote, cheap places are very remote, as well as unstimulating. Suburbs of cities are full of distractions. Children need education, doctors, and, frequently, shoes, as well as love. Standard typewriters are hellish as baggage. I speak frivolously, but the croppers we nearly came were as much for frivolous reasons as major ones. There are a thousand drains on your resources, inner and physical.

But at the end of seven years of it, there was a sense of tremendous fulfillment, contentment, and the wonder of the rainbow over Gibraltar.

Still, "It's not what you do, it's what you are that counts," Wert said.

It was not surprising that, at the end, he found Montaigne his most sympathetic reading.

"People are wrong," says Montaigne "Of Experience." "It is much easier to go along the sides where the far edge serves as a limit and a guide, than by the middle way, which is broad and open, and to go by art, than by nature; but it is also much less noble and commendable. Greatness of soul is not so much mounting high and pressing forward, as knowing how to put oneself in order and circumscribe oneself. It regards as great all that is enough and shows its elevation by preferring moderate things to eminent ones. There is nothing as beautiful and just as to play the man well and fitly, nor any knowledge so arduous as to know how to live this life well and naturally; and of all our maladies the most barbarous is to despise our being."

Wert refused to despise his flesh, even now. He would call me over and, spending time at it, we would touch faces and mouths as boys and girls do. What freshness and sweetness there was in that kissing, in the touching of faces above his ruined body.

"It's like it was, now there's nothing else. Virginal," he said. "How good it is. How sweet. How good it was when you were young."

He smoked his black cigarettes with immense, conscious pleasure, now that food and drink were impossible to him. After the sixtieth cigarette one night, he burst into laughter. "I certainly fooled hell out of the lung cancer boys," he said joyously.

An immoderate man in all things, he had come to his "arduous knowledge" and to the control of himself which gave him a measure of control over his life and his *hubris* not by moderation but by balance and harmony: between his rebellions and his ambitions; between happiness and honor; indulgence and discipline—among work, love, and enjoyment. It was a serene equation.

As a hoper, not a dreamer, he left his world, having found it imperfect and good, hopeful for it, hoping that the best he had been would live after him.

His mistakes were done with, too, the ones he had made as a political man, as a social man, the lacks he felt in himself as a thinking man. From the day we had known he would die, we had never mentioned politics because our sense of immediacy disappeared. We had not mentioned religion, although we had concerned ourselves in the past with the problems of both faith and faiths. "It would be mighty interesting to be a mystic right now," he said once, "but I'm not and I never could take anything second hand."

"We are closer together than I thought two people could

ever be," he said to me near the end. "I look for you and you are there. It's the most I've wanted."

"I'll settle for it," he said, looking back over the whole. He was dying without frustration, letting his life go, at fifty-three, letting the past, me, his children, the years he had planned, go. "It's damned hard for a man to tell right from wrong," he said, "but it's easy to tell good from evil."

16

"Bad to worse to worst" read the note in the *carnet* almost illegibly on December 26th, and at five o'clock Wert said what I had known with interior tension he would say: "Time's come."

"Are you afraid?" I asked him.

"Mmmm hum," he admitted.

I wanted to plead with him for one more day, but I did not. A brief *crise* in the early evening made me glad I had not. We went upstairs at ten. It was very cold, but there was no wind. I had kept the electric heaters on all day in both the bathroom and the bedroom and the rooms were quite warm. Ama had given over protesting my extravagance and no longer pulled the plugs out to save me money when I was not looking. She had put boiling-hot-water bottles in our two beds. We undressed and waited until the house was deeply quiet except for Ama's audible snoring in the room above ours, where she slept with Timberlake. They slept like rocks. Chris, who was easier to awaken, had his room on the other side of the hall and stairwell on the third floor. Wert read over the pamphlet on morphine again while I went down and boiled water and all the hypodermics we had.

"Silly, when we are sterile and when we aren't," Wert remarked. On the ship we had not bothered. Later we did.

Carefully he refigured his possible tolerance of morphine

acquired from the doses he had allowed himself when no other drugs were effective. First, he gave himself a small shot; I believe this was designed to avoid the danger of nausea. While he was waiting twenty minutes, he took his copy of Montaigne, with old bullfight tickets stuck in it for markers where he had particularly responded to certain pages, and dated it and wrote in it a message for John Hersey, to whom I was to send it. Then he took the white pills he had counted out and we made a solution of them which, as he stirred it, turned perfectly clear and looked like water.

"Here goes," he said, and began pumping the big doses into his leg. His hand shook. He bent and broke one needle, but rescued the liquid, saying, "Damn it! Don't let me make a mess of this."

With twelve grains of morphine, he was theoretically sure, but for good measure he gave himself three more. Then he lay back on the pillow and I sat beside him and held his hands. "I love you and I've had a damned fine life," he said, and closed his eyes in an exhaustion like death.

In a minute he opened one eye. "Purple haze coming as promised," he said, "but 'we cain't do nothin' till Martin gits here!' . . ."

In another minute the eye opened again and then the other one and he said, "A gentleman should know when to take his leave." A long, deep look . . . and then he seemed to go out.

Sometimes it seemed to me his heart beat fast and sometimes very slowly, but it continued to beat strongly. His breathing varied from very slow and gasping to quick and shallow. His hands seemed still conscious of holding mine. I don't know how long it was until he opened both eyes and said, sounding indignant, "I'm not going to die. I feel sheepish."

A little later I brought him a red casserole and he staggered to his feet, weaving. For some reason, he had taken the hot-water bottle which had been behind his shoulderblades and put it on his head. Holding the red casserole in both hands made the stance of the male performing this office even more exaggerated. He looked at my expression and began to laugh and I laughed too. It was not hysterical, but real laughter.

"It's funny," agreed Wert, "but damn it all, woman, do you realize that what I am peeing away contains valuable morphine?"

He was wholly free of pain, clear-headed and wakeful. Settling himself comfortably, for he'd had the most trouble getting comfortable lying down for days, he told me to pull up the armchair in place of my backless footstool. We stayed thus and talked until five in the morning, when he went to sleep. It was a lovely night.

The next day he could not get down the stairs. I telephoned Steve in Paris. "He took enough to kill an elephant," I said to Steve, "and all it did was make him feel good. What a man." It was foolish but I felt proud as well as intensely worried. "But today's rough, and we used a big hunk of our American supply last night, and this thing's getting unbearable, you know. The other kind of morphine works better for pain, so he wants to try it tonight. But, Steve, if we use too much, and it doesn't work, we may run into terrible trouble. Can you find out what went wrong? Can you get and send down some more? I've some French friends who can get a little in Bordeaux, but . . ." "He's got to be able to kill himself when he wants to," said Steve. "My God. I'll find out everything I can, get everything I can. What about sleeping pills?" "He says they're for dames," I said. "He wouldn't want to use them even if he could, but he can't anyway because he can't keep anything down he swallows. Solves that problem." "I'll call you back," said Steve, who had seen Wert for a few minutes when a *crise* just bypassed him, and whose heart was in his voice.

Wert tried again the night of the 27th with vials of French morphine solution. We had a feeling this morphine was more effective and might work. We proceeded as before, and the moments were equally intense. If I quote him jesting it is not to offer, or because he offered it as, comedy relief. We were a long way beyond any self-consciousness and if he thought of something for his or our amusement, he said it. Such things are isolated in memory from the rest, being separate and sharp.

In the small hours of the night before, after he did not die, he had said, "Lo, the poor idiom." I had promised to send it on to his son Bill, and to Suzie and Frances Ann, all admirers of his puns.

"I'm running out of last words," he said before this second try. "Make a list and take your choice. But *don't* forget my last pun."

As he passed out, into a deep, slow-breathing unconsciousness, he murmured, "I love you," and I thought they were truly his last.

After an hour or so his breathing, though still slow and very heavy, no longer stopped at intervals, and I knew he was not going to die this time, either. I went through an agonized half hour trying to decide whether to give him any more. That was what he wanted me to do, if it would make the difference, if he was almost and not quite out. I could not, and so I went to bed and slept myself, clutching at unconsciousness until we could be conscious together again.

Next morning he wrote in his *carnet:* "Tried again. No go. Slept." During the day, he felt "not so bad."

"I couldn't," I told him then. "I'd have done anything you said absolutely to do, but I *couldn't* decide for you by myself. I couldn't give you another dose that might have done it or might just not have and been worse . . ."

"You shouldn't have. You were right," he said. "Entirely right not to."

"Besides, I wanted you to go out peacefully like that, but oh, I'm so glad you're here another day. I'm so grateful for having you."

"Staunch," said Wert, using with perception the one word that wiped out my feeling that I had been selfish or cowardly or somehow lacking. "Let's let it go for three days if we can. Too much emotion. New Year's Eve, now. That would be ceremonial. I'd rather like that. Lay in a bottle of the best champagne."

Better, he dressed and was downstairs by noon. He tried to eat, choosing a dry, not-too-sweet cookie, but it didn't work. We had a scare when he gave in and took two grains of morphine and it gave him no reaction, but the next dose relieved him. Steve telephoned and said he'd found an American-trained doctor who suggested, after due double-talk, that even fifteen grains of morphine might not work if the subject were insufficiently relaxed. We should combine it with soporifics. He had stuff for us and would send it on the Sud-Express by some passenger I should meet in Bayonne at the station unless he could locate a Basque train porter whom he could trust. From the Paris station, he would telephone and tell me for whom I was to look.

A friendly young couple were hanging out the window looking for me from Steve's description of me when the train pulled in. The package in my hands, I thanked them, without ever knowing their names.

New Year's Eve midnight, with champagne in hollow-stemmed, chilled glasses we touched and drank a little from, he made his ceremonial try. Again, this time combining the morphine with four 100-mgm. Nembutal suppositories to get the relaxation the doctor we did not know had recommended, he went off into a sleep, almost before he could finish getting the shots in, his hand shaking with haste and weakness. Sometimes he stopped breathing for as long as two minutes. Next day, January 1st, 1955, he wrote "Happy New Year!" in the *carnet*.

"There is always cutting the wrists," he said wearily. "I'd like to put that off as long as I can. Messy. Hard on you."

Each day was a kind of miracle of his being there and each day claimed from him an exorbitant price. His handwriting, which had been scraggly and nearly illegible for a while, came sharp and clear again as he headed the pages left for NOTES at the end of 1954's fillers with the dates in 1955 so that he could leave the new year's pages fresh for Chris to put into the cover. "Monday—3rd. Weary from no sleep. No eat. Lunch puts anyway. Bach. Good day between times." "Tuesday—4th. Getting mighty low. Bath. Music. My love." "Wed.—5th. Terrible night. Worst day yet. Play bubbles game. No go."

The "bubbles game" was his attempt to insert an air bubble into a vein. Wert remembered a news story of a murder committed in some French province in which the murderer, a doctor, had pumped an air bubble into the vein of his victim. I remembered a Marquand novel and an old mystery story that used this means. Wert spent the 5th engrossed in trying to manage it.

During the first hour he would call to me with excitement whenever he succeeded in getting a needle into a vein, which proved to be difficult enough. Once he thought he'd actually forced in several cubic centimeters of air. We speculated wildly on what happened next if he had.

Late in the afternoon, he said, "Damn it, you don't seem to be taking this quite seriously."

"I'd be 'ever so surprised' if it worked," I admitted. "I think it takes an expert."

"Well, you wouldn't begrudge a man his limited amusements, would you?" said Wert. "Keeps me occupied, anyway."

"I feel better about every damn human being in the whole world because you are a man," I said, and he said, "What a nice thing to say."

I'd have been glad enough if the bubbles had worked. I helped all I could. The dope problem, in spite of Cartier, Steve, and what we had left from the U.S. and Bordeaux, was getting grim. The day before, Cartier had told me the only thing left to do was to give Wert a shot in the spine, which was "dangerous," but which would paralyze him from the waist down temporarily and provide sure relief. "Body in bed," said Wert to me. "No control over functions. No."

The page for the 6th, in spite of a steady heading and two careful notes on his shots, is scribbled. I can only make out the words: "We have every . . . End hoped and tried for . . ."

On the 7th, by the fire, he said: "That's the last time I can make those stairs. I can't hear music any more. I can't drink even tea. The cigarettes taste bad. I'm only staying alive to see your face."

It had to be that night, if it was to be his way, and we both knew it. We waited until very late, talking together with a kind of final serenity unmatched at any other time. He planned everything most carefully, aware that nothing was as you planned it, but with determination that however and whatever, he must die. Debating the amount in case it should make him too shaky, he took a small last shot of morphine. I brought his Rolls razor, freshly stropped, and he detached the blade.

I couldn't watch when he cut, or as he went in again—when the flow into the red casseroles, on which he rested his wrists so that the blood wouldn't spill on the bed and the floor, slowed and stopped—although I had to hold him up then. Then the cancer seemed to rouse and to fight him, as if evil were fighting for its own life, which would die with his. I started pumping morphine into him, cutting my fingers a little on the glass tubes I was breaking as fast as I could, so that our blood mingled for an instant, symbol of all love. He was afraid of crying out and waking the children and I begged him to pass out and promised him he would die whatever I had to do and he said, "Quick, a towel, I'm losing control," and I got a towel between his legs. I said, "I love you I love you please die," and he said that one first phrase, too, and went into the final struggle to die and did.

The wax and bones of him I got between clean sheets and into clean white silk pajamas, and I bound the ragged wrists in flesh-colored adhesive tape as he planned for me to do. Although only Dominique that night would see him, he lay in dignity and cleanliness. Then it was time to wake and send Ama out into the 3:00 A.M. rain for Dominique to help me dress him, which I could not do alone. In the morning, there were his children to wake, each one, and tell and comfort them. There were the doctor, the mayor, the undertaker, to see. There were the cables to send across the ocean, as he had asked me to, and the quick, traditional visits of the Basques, who said, "Life goes on, Mommy, that's how it is." Then there was time to mourn the death of a man.